LETTING GO

NCTE Editorial Board

Letting Go

*How to Give Your Students
Control over Their Learning
in the English Classroom*

Meg Donhauser
Hunterdon Central Regional High School, Flemington, New Jersey

Cathy Stutzman
Hunterdon Central Regional High School, Flemington, New Jersey

Heather Hersey
Lakeside School, Seattle, Washington

National Council of Teachers of English
1111 W. Kenyon Road, Urbana, Illinois 61801-1096

Staff Editor: Bonny Graham

Manuscript Editor: The Charlesworth Group

Interior Design: Jenny Jensen Greenleaf

Cover Design: Pat Mayer

Cover Image: Kesu01/iStock/Thinkstock

NCTE Stock Number: 28046; eStock Number: 28060
ISBN 978-0-8141-2804-6; eISBN 978-0-8141-2806-0

Library of Congress Cataloging-in-Publication Data

Names: Donhauser, Meg, 1983- author. | Stutzman, Cathy, 1979- author. |
    Hersey, Heather, 1971- author.
Title: Letting go : how to give your students control over their learning in the English
    classroom / Meg Donhauser, Hunterdon Central Regional High School; Cathy
    Stutzman, Hunterdon Central Regional High School; Heather Hersey, Lakeside
    School.
Description: Urbana, Illinois : National Council of Teachers of English, [2018] | Includes
    bibliographical references and index.
Identifiers: LCCN 2018009120 (print) | LCCN 2018025402 (ebook) | ISBN 9780814128060
    (ebook) | ISBN 9780814128046 (pbk.))
Subjects: LCSH: Inquiry-based learning. | Student participation in curriculum planning.
    | Students—Self-rating of. | Language arts.
Classification: LCC LB1027.23 (ebook) | LCC LB1027.23 .D66 2018 (print) | DDC
    371.39—dc23
LC record available at https://lccn.loc.gov/2018009120

To all of our students—past, present, and future—keep asking questions!

Contents

Foreword

WILL RICHARDSON

L etting go" is such an appropriate sentiment for this moment in education. The fact is that learning, like Elvis, has left the building. That's not to say that schools have been the only places in which learning has occurred in the past. But today, because of the internet and the tools we use to access it, learning can happen anywhere, at any time, with anyone. And, most important, learners themselves are in charge of the process. They pursue their own questions and interests, build their own curricula, find their own teachers, and assess their own progress. They decide the scope, the sequence, and the pace.

That shift from the institution to the individual is arguably the most profound educational shift ever. That's a big statement, I know. But think about the incredible challenges schools now must face if they are to adequately prepare students to thrive in the new global, networked, always on, complex learning environment we all are now living in. Think about the new skills, the new literacies, and the important dispositions that our children must develop in order to make sense of and take full advantage of it. And think of how different learning outside of school looks from learning inside of school today. If you have kids, or grandkids, or spend time with kids, you know what I'm talking about. Find a nine-year-old who plays *Minecraft* and ask her how she learned it and you'll immediately understand.

The irony is that, as a society, we seem to be attempting to deal with this shift in exactly the wrong way. We want more curriculum, more time in school, more assessments, more control, when, in reality, we should be doing less of all of that. If the purpose of school is to create kids who know a lot of stuff (that they'll quickly forget) and who can get high test scores (that tell little about what is actually learned), then, sure, take that approach. But, in a world where content and teachers and technologies are increasingly abundant, the purpose of school must now be to develop the most powerful, literate, just-in-time learners we can, not just-in-case knowers.

To do that—to create the most opportune conditions in schools for our kids to develop as learners—we must let go. We must create classrooms and schoolhouses that support and celebrate true learning autonomy for students, ones in which they have real choice over what they learn, how they learn it, and how they show they've learned it. In the words of Stephen Downes (2011), "We need to move beyond the idea that an education is something that is provided for us, and toward the idea that an education is something that we create for ourselves" (para. 21). Or, in this context, that learners create for themselves. More them, less us. Much less.

This will not be an easy transition to make. Schools as institutions are painfully difficult to change because the people who run them (and the people who send their kids to them) are products of that institution. "School" is familiar to us. It's ingrained in the story that we tell about childhood. And deviating from the story, regardless of how effective, or ineffective, it may be, does not make us comfortable.

So where do we start? How do we begin to change our practice in ways that move more agency over learning to students yet help them achieve those traditional outcomes that, for now at least, are required for getting over those institutional bars?

Happily, if you're reading this, you've chosen to start here, with this great book by three former colleagues and, importantly, teachers of my own kids. As a high school English teacher who worked alongside Cathy, Meg, and Heather, I know from firsthand experience the passion they bring to this work, and the deep desire they have to make sure all of their students become powerful learners for the world as it is, not as it was for most of us.

As you'll soon find out, the *inquiry learning plan* (ILP) that they have created and that they detail in this book is such a great tool for teachers who are seeking to move further down the path to student agency yet might not feel comfortable or clear about a path that may seem even more "risky" in terms of traditional outcomes. Their own inquiry in the introduction sets the table neatly: "How can we encourage students to love reading, writing, and learning while also meeting the demands of testing and preparing students for an unsure world?"

That's an important question that all of us in education should be asking today. Unfortunately, however, it's a question that not enough of us are asking. This book is chock-full of strategies and examples that will guide teachers at any level to answer that question in ways that can make a profound impact on their students, as shown by the numerous student testimonials the authors include. It's a deep dive into how to best create a powerful learning experience for kids that lets them own the process, develops them as independent learners, and ensures they are "successful" in terms of the outcomes and expectations that are outside of their control.

Honestly, I'm only half kidding when I say I wish I'd invented the ILP first.

It would have had a great impact on my students when I was in the classroom, and it would have helped me understand more deeply the kinds of changes that are required in our practice in this fast-changing moment.

Sincerely, I know you'll enjoy *Letting Go*. I know you'll learn a lot about learning and teaching that makes sense for the modern world. And, most important, I know your students will be better prepared to learn their way into their futures because of it.

Acknowledgments

This book has been five years in the making, with its creation and contributions spanning from coast to coast. There have been so many people with kind words, questions, and excitement, and we wish we could thank each one of you individually. Certainly, we would be remiss if we did not thank the following people for their exceptional (and often time-consuming) contributions to this book:

- Brendan McIsaac, for challenging and questioning us—you made the ILP so much better and gave us the courage to share our work!

- Brien Gorham, for guidance, breakfasts, patience, calming us down when we needed it, and propping us up all the time

- our pets—we're sorry for every missed walk and pet as we worked on this book: Ember, Jack, Juliet, Lucky, and Scout

- our families and friends for your patience and encouragement

- Will Richardson, for providing publishing guidance and support, for trusting Meg to teach his daughter with the ILP, for his consistent work and passion around education, and for contributing the foreword to this book

- Dr. Bill Fernekes, our comrade, for giving us the confidence to move forward with this project and his support along the way

- Marci Zane, for beginning this journey with us, always asking questions, thinking deeply, and encouraging us to keep going

- Michael Smith, for his time, coaching, and inspiration—thank you for encouraging us to "tell [you] more"

- Carol Kuhlthau, for her research about the information search process, especially the affective domain of student learning, which has been so influential for us

- for using the ILP and allowing us to share your work here: Dan Butler, Lindsay Warren, Suzanne Vrancken, and Erin Sollner

- to others who tried the ILP, allowed us to observe classes, and are referenced throughout this book

- Melinda McBee Orzulak for encouraging us to write a book

- for reading, editing, and providing valuable feedback: Mary Woods, Cindy Forck, Sarah Reichenbecher, Melissa Mongi, Melissa Stager, and Ruth Donhauser

- Bonny Graham, for answering our relentless emails, for appreciating our meticulousness, and for helping us to shape our ideas. Thank you and NCTE for believing in this project from the beginning and bringing it to publication!

- Google Drive and Hangouts, thank you for arriving just in time to support this project. Coast-to-coast collaboration would have been extremely challenging without you!

- Cocco's and Factory Fuel Company in Flemington, NJ—thank you for the comfy seats and caffeine.

And, of course, to all of our students who were brave enough to try this, who inspired us to be better teachers, and who taught us new things every day, thank you.

Introduction

So . . . Why Do You Want to Be an English Teacher?

You were likely asked this question by someone as you were preparing to be a teacher, and, depending on the tone, it may have been from a reflective professor or an incredulous friend. Think back . . . what was your answer? Maybe it had something to do with igniting a love of writing in your students, or encouraging a passion for literature, or helping students become "lifelong learners." A teacher with goals like these would never hear one of her students say, "Please don't ruin *The Catcher in the Rye* for me . . . it's my favorite book." But it happened to one of us, despite having every opposite intention.

Now think about the comments you hear from your colleagues. Are they talking about how students can't stop loving Shakespeare? Or literary analysis essays? Not likely. In fact, we sometimes hear the reverse—accounts of unmotivated or grade-motivated students going through the motions with no hint of the love we so want them to have. These days it is easy to blame testing and standards, but, if we're honest, and this book will show you that we were, it is often us and our inability to let go of things such as content and order that leave our students feeling like the subject we love is just one more hoop for them to jump through.

Imagine today's teacher, who has the responsibility of choosing from centuries of writing across hundreds of cultures. How can she possibly be sure that she is selecting "the best" or what is most needed by her students? Furthermore, many of the skill-based lessons she does reach only a part of the class perfectly. Some students are bored because they already know how to do it, while, for others, the skill is too advanced to be meaningful. She also sometimes feels like she is limiting students' learning to only what she knows well, and, with honest reflection, realizes that this leaves out a lot, some of which might be more in line with her students' passions. Just as she is afraid to take risks with what and how she teaches, her students are afraid to take risks in what and how they learn—a very dangerous way to think in our constantly changing world. She really desires a better way to connect learning more deeply to her students' interests and to the outside world while still meeting standards and preparing students for their postsecondary lives. She feels frustrated because the way she was taught doesn't seem to fit anymore, but she doesn't know what to do.

So what is the answer? How can we encourage students to love reading, writing, and learning while also meeting the demands of testing and preparing them for an unsure world—and don't forget maintaining our own sanity! There are practitioners who provide methods with which to address some of these challenges:

- Penny Kittle (2012) and Nancie Atwell (1987) showed us how to give students a choice of texts, igniting a love for reading.
- Chris Lehmann (2013) and the faculty at the Science Leadership Academy demonstrated that, through project-based learning, students can solve real-world problems while collaborating and connecting with community.
- Will Richardson (2012) advocated for the use of technology to expand the breadth of expertise to which students are exposed.
- Carol Kuhlthau's (2004) *information search process* (ISP) taught us how to approach research with attention to the emotional responses students may face while learning.
- Kathleen Cushman (2010) used surveys as a way for teachers to honor student interests and create an inspired classroom community.

Combining all of these options seems overwhelming. Choosing one might solve some of the problems we face, but doesn't cover them all.

The best option for us has been to "let go and let inquiry"—focusing our teaching around student-generated questions, and then allowing students to lead, find their own way, and discover their own passions. That's why we created our own approach, inspired by the incredible work of the practitioners above and many others. We used our understanding of those best practices and combined them with our own teaching experience to develop the *inquiry learning plan* (hereafter, ILP), an organizational tool that allows students to experience the inquiry process and guide their learning.

The ILP

Basically, the ILP is a customizable tool that allows for teacher and student collaboration and communication as students take responsibility for aspects of their learning. Though it has gone through many revisions, when Meg first created the ILP, she was inspired by Wiggins and McTighe's (2005) *Understanding by Design*, which focuses on a planning method called "backward design":

> An approach to designing a curriculum or unit that begins with the end in mind and designs toward that end.... [I]t is viewed as backward because many teachers begin their unit design with the means—textbooks, favored lessons, and time-honored activities—rather than deriving those from the end—the targeted results, such as content standards or understandings. (p. 338)

Meg took this philosophy and thought, "Why not allow students to devise their own learning?" As a firm believer in student-centered, student-led classrooms, she decided to let students engineer their own learning plans rather than follow a predetermined path from the teacher—and the ILP was born.

The ILP offers both the freedom and the structure to guide your students to success. Through a series of activities and reflections that culminate in a final learning artifact, the ILP elevates individualization of content, skills, and dispositions as students become the architects of their own learning. Most of the strategies in this book can be used individually; however, we will also explain how they fit into the ILP process. When we teach professional development classes about inquiry, we generally start with a preview of the ILP and a description of each section. This helps to set the tone and give participants a visual prior to digging into the strategies.

As you can see in Figure 1, the ILP is divided into four sections, beginning with students outlining the materials they will be studying and ending with a final project called "So what?" Next, we give a brief overview of the ILP's sections, and each chapter will dive in more deeply.

- *Section One: What I will read.* Though the ILP process can also start with questions or standards depending on your goals, we've placed a list of texts first, charting what students will be studying. This first section could be approached in any way. Most frequently, we use theme, literary movement, or genre. Depending on the unit length and course needs, you can determine the requirements for this section, including how much choice students have in the texts they use.

What I Will Read

List the core materials below.

List resources below that will aid your inquiry.

What I Will Learn

Please list your essential and guiding questions that you plan on pursuing this unit.

Please list all standards that you intend on practicing this unit. Remember, choose standards that you have not already mastered since you will have to demonstrate that you are getting better as the unit progresses.

Student Growth: The Learning Process and Reflections

Learning Activities: Throughout the course of the unit, you will complete nine activities. By the end of the ILP, you will be synthesizing what you've learned about your texts and research to help you better understand the essential questions, and all of the standards must be addressed at least once in each round.

Activity 1:

Activity 2:

Activity 3:

EQ Reflection 1: How do your texts and research help you answer your questions? What do you still need to learn?

Standards Reflection 1: What progress have you made toward your standards? What do you still need to learn?

(Students will repeat the process of three activities, an EQ Reflection, and a Standards Reflection multiple times.)

So What?: The Outcomes

Now that you've developed your skills, learned new information, and gained insights, what are you going to do? This final project should be influenced by the work you've completed these past few weeks.

- First, determine what the main lesson of this unit is. What is your take-away in terms of the texts, standards, and essential questions? Then, decide who needs to know about what you've learned. Is there an important skill or lesson you want to share with others? Find an authentic audience and articulate why this person or group of people are the best audience for your lesson. What means will you use to communicate your discoveries?
- Develop a rationale for your project in which you'll discuss how your work has inspired you. Using your texts and standards, explain what you'll do for your project in the space below.
- Finally, create the product that you've outlined in your rationale and share it with your audience!

Marginal annotations:

In this first section, students list the various texts and resources that they will explore throughout the unit. We have divided these texts into core and supplementary materials.

It is important to push students in areas where they need improvement. We stress to them that they cannot simply showcase what they are good at, and the point of the class is to practice skills that they need to improve. We try to stress growth more than anything.

The reflections are a synthesis of the content and skills students learned through the activities. The EQ reflection should focus around the answers a student has developed. Both reflections allow students to determine what their next steps will be; what questions do they now have about the topic? In terms of standards, what do they still need to improve?

Here we stress the importance of divergent questions that speak to students' genuine interests. Prior to selecting a question, students need to explore the topic. In our case, that might be reading a short text or two from the genre or literary era we're studying.

Each activity is designed to address a standard. In the learning plan, students write out the directions for the activity they create. Students complete multiple activities per standard to show their growth in that skill over time.

This is the final artifact of the students' learning. Here, students draw up a proposal that shows how they will incorporate both the skills they attained and the content they learned during the course of the unit.

FIGURE 1. ILP with section explanations. Adapted from "From Lesson Plan to Learning Plan: An Introduction to the Inquiry Learning Plan," by M. Donhauser, H. Hersey, C. Stutzman, and M. Zane, 2014a, *School Library Monthly* (an imprint of ABC-CLIO), *31*(1), p. 13. CC BY-NC-SA.

- *Section Two: What I will learn.* The next aspect of the ILP serves as a plan for the student's discovery and mastery. Here, students will list essential and guiding questions (referred to hereafter as EQs and GQs, respectively) and will choose their standards for the unit. As stated earlier, the questions can be developed before, after, or in conjunction with choosing texts, but it is imperative that students have a record of their questions not only to share with the teacher and their peers but also to help them focus their inquiry. It's exciting for students to see how texts inform questions and questions invite new texts!

- *Section Three: Student growth.* In this section of the ILP, students direct how they learn new information and practice the standards as they design and complete rounds of activities and reflections that show growth in terms of skills and content knowledge. Through these activities, students also demonstrate that they are actively trying to answer the EQs and GQs of the unit. This section is where the magic happens as students make discoveries about not just what they are learning but also about *how* they are learning it.

- *Section Four: "So what?"* The "So what?" section brings their learning together and out beyond the walls of the classroom. Using the reflections, students determine the most compelling takeaway of the unit or course. It may be an answer to the EQ or a skill that the student feels is necessary for success; it will be as individualized as the rest of the learning plan. We start talking about this final step when we introduce reflections for the first time, since students should begin thinking about the deeper meanings and bigger implications of their EQs. This is a fundamental shift from backward design. Instead of students working toward a predetermined end product, the "So what?" element becomes a natural extension of learning, allowing students to think carefully about the content and skills in order to choose the best way to express what they've learned.

Clearly, the ILP is a living document, one that is constantly being updated as students read and research, practice skills, complete reflections, and collaborate with other learners. It allows you to provide specific, ongoing feedback and for students to develop skills in areas that are most meaningful to them. One tenth-grade student wrote in an anonymous reflection:

I loved getting a choice of books and a choice of activities. I felt like my brain was taken out of its little box and allowed to roam free and explore when we got choices besides the boring, repetitive, recurring essay format.

Because of its customizable nature, the ILP remains adaptable enough for you to use regardless of curricular requirements, enabling you to "let go" of content, skills, and assessment, or a combination of them, in an organized way. Let's be real though . . . letting go is scary and sometimes challenging, for a variety of reasons. Turning over control is especially tricky in districts where student-driven learning, shared responsibility, and a general culture of inquiry are not already fostered or supported. Furthermore, some school or course requirements may not allow teachers the autonomy to restructure their classes. Even for teachers who do have that support and freedom, there is intense pressure to "cover" so much for tests, for college, for life. As we contemplated shifting our practices to put more control in our students' hands, we had to come to terms with the fact that we wouldn't always know where our students' explorations would take them. We had to let go of them knowing the symbols or themes that we used to teach and let go of the comfort that comes with knowing we are directing students toward a predetermined endpoint. We can honestly say that it's been worth it!

Our use of the ILP varies according to the needs of the class. In our most individualized classes, students choose independent reads, develop their own questions, select standards-based skills that they will practice, create activities and assessments, reflect on their learning, and share their greatest takeaways authentically. We knew that, if we wanted to pursue this structure, we would have to develop strategies that enable us and other teachers to choose how much to let go and in what ways. This was a challenging and exciting process, and we've spent years developing and refining this approach with input from other teachers, students, administrators, education consultants, teacher–librarians, and parents. Now we're ready to share what we've learned through this book, with the main purposes of (a) demonstrating that letting go is a rewarding experience and (b) breaking down the strategies and processes that support a gradual release of responsibility to students.

How We Got Here

We began our teaching transformation with two important questions: Why do we assume the texts we traditionally teach are more valuable than others, and how do we decide what is the most important aspect of a subject that a student should explore? As Meg and Cathy were pondering these questions, they were involved in a one-to-one computing pilot alongside Heather, where they learned about our changing world and how a traditional curriculum no longer prepares students adequately for the future. It was during this pilot that Heather and another librarian, Marci Zane, introduced Meg to the idea of inquiry as found in the teacher-librarian field. As a group, we learned about how the ubiquitous availability of information required a shift in the role of teachers and librarians from delivering content to helping students find, create, and share information while accessing tools to improve their organization and track their progress. The serendipitous culmination of our questions, our focus on inquiry, and the student-led learning focus of the one-to-one pilot brought us to where we are now. However, the road was not always smooth: it was and is still filled with questions.

But Aren't You the Teacher?

As we began to use these methods in our classrooms, one of the biggest questions from students was, "Why can't you just teach us?" To increase their perseverance, we had to learn how to communicate our reasons very clearly to help students understand that, though this type of learning might feel different, we are still actually teaching. Weimer (2014) described this phenomenon in her blog post for *Faculty Focus*:

> This is a style of teaching that promotes learning, but that's not how students see it. Based on experiences in lots of other classrooms, they have come to believe that "good" teachers tell students what they need to know. If a teacher makes the students come up with examples when she has a perfectly good list she could be giving them, that teacher is not doing her job. (para. 2)

Therefore, teachers need to not only monitor the feelings of students but also of themselves. Weimer (2014) made a key discovery that is significant when working with the ILP: "If teachers are going to refuse to do something students expect, especially if students think it's something they believe makes the learning easier, how teachers refuse to help is important" (para. 6). Breaking students from their reliance on a more passive type of learning is difficult and doesn't work without clear communication. It is a process that requires practice and patience on the part of teachers and students.

This is where discussions of inquiry learning from the school library field are essential. We used Kuhlthau's (2004) ISP because of her focus on the affective domain (see Figure 2). Teaching students about how inquiry learning "feels" is one of the ways to help students prepare for this type of work. We needed to scaffold the process and understand how their feelings throughout the process affected their learning. Kuhlthau's (2004) ISP illustrated not only the thoughts and actions of people as they research but also how they're feeling.

Though the ILP is not exclusively a research tool, students experience many of the same feelings of frustration and doubt while using it. Showing them the process that successful researchers go through, with all of the ups and downs that the process contains, helps students to understand that learning should be messy. It shows them that the feelings Kuhlthau (2004) identified—being "uncomfortable," "frustrated," and even "doubtful"—are simply part of the process and mean that they're doing a good job learning. We also explain to them that the discomfort eases once they have more experience with this type of learning. The more they go through the process, the more they begin to trust it. This can be seen in a number of the anonymous end-of-the-year reflections, such as this one:

> At first, I was really hesitant about the structure of this class and honestly didn't feel like I would learn anything useful since it was not like the structure of a normal English class. However, having concluded this course, I feel as though I surprised myself as to what I was capable of and learned more than I expected to that relates to real life and myself. I came to really like the structure because it allowed me to shine in MY strengths and improve in MY weaknesses which I really felt [was] helpful in my learning process.

Model of the Information Search Process						
	Initiation	Selection	Exploration	Formulation	Collection	Presentation	Assessment
Feelings (Affective)	Uncertainty	Optimism	Confusion Frustration Doubt	Clarity	Sense of direction / Confidence	Satisfaction or Disappointment	Sense of accomplishment
Thoughts (Cognitive)	vague ⟶			focused	increased	interest	Increased self-awareness
Actions (Physical)	seeking	relevant Exploring	information	seeking	pertinent Documenting	information	

FIGURE 2. Model of the ISP. Reproduced from *Seeking Meaning: A Process Approach to Library and Information Services* (2nd ed., p. 82), by C. C. Kuhlthau, 2004, Westport, CT: Libraries Unlimited. Reproduced with permission.

This Sounds Difficult . . . Why Should I Try It?

Though we began in different places, our convictions about this type of learning were the same. So we came together to consider what students should be able to do as a result of their experiences in our classes and devised three outcomes that have remained our guideposts throughout this process. Students should be able to:

1. ask and answer questions using appropriate texts, personal experiences, and one another

2. assess their strengths and weaknesses and execute a plan to improve on those skills

3. build an awareness of their role in their community and what they can offer to others.

These skills transcend disciplines and help prepare students for life, not just college. The ILP creates opportunities for students to build "habits of mind" such as self-direction, adaptability, and a tolerance for ambiguity (see also Costa, 2008), in addition to critical skills like literacy, communication, and collaboration. They experience and begin to get comfortable with the discomfort of learning. As Jen, a twelfth-grade student explained:

> I have never been in a class where I sort of was a teacher to myself. I got to choose what I read, what I studied, what I focused on, what I was able to do as work, and what my guidelines were. I have always been in a class where teachers told me what I had to do and when. So this class sort of made me grow up. I was given deadlines for a product, but I needed to do everything on my own. I feel like this class stressed responsibility in an individual, which I feel will definitely help me next, when I am a college freshman and really on my own. The responsibility for my own work will definitely transfer out of this class and follow me in everyday tasks, whether it is for school, a job, or just in interpersonal affairs. This process of gaining responsibility was the most important part of my journey.

In classrooms where the teacher makes most of the decisions, this response is not likely. As we used the ILP, we learned that we must let go of our past roles, but we also learned about the new roles that students will take up when we let go. They become teachers of themselves, their peers, and us, and they become stronger, more self-reliant learners. This is why we do it. If using the ILP had just remained a theoretical promise, we would not advocate for it. It is the changes we've seen in students and how they learn that make this type of student-led learning worthwhile.

Another hallmark of the ILP is its focus on the transfer of knowledge and skills by using cycles of activities and reflection. As students move through the ILP, they are consistently creating and revising questions, learning new knowledge and skills, reevaluating where they are, and reflecting on their progress. Its beauty is its ability not only to individualize learning, but also to enable students to discover their learning and for us to see more deeply into their progress and process. In essence, we see the thinking that takes the student from questions to answers to more questions. Along with the student, you will be able to trace learning through various stages, enabling you to get to know your students even better as learners and for your students to know themselves.

As Cushman (2010) explained, there are great rewards for embarking on this type of learning:

> When adults openly explore genuine questions about getting to mastery—and include young people's knowledge and experiences in that exploration—we model the expert's habit of taking intellectual and creative risks. We demonstrate that we too always have things we need to understand better, and things we need to practice. We teach kids to approach any lack of understanding as a puzzle: stretching the limits of their competence, continually testing new possibilities, and seeing how they work out. As they expand their knowledge and skills, young people, like us, will discover even more challenging puzzles they want to tackle—not just outside of school but as part of it. (p. 10)

The setup of the ILP encourages this puzzle approach to learning because it allows for consistent reflection upon and modification of the questions that students begin with. The futurist writer Alvin Toffler was quoted as saying, "The illiterate of the twenty-first century will not be those who cannot read and write, but those who cannot learn, unlearn, and relearn" (qtd. in Crockett, Jukes, & Churches, 2011, p. 17). For students to reach this level of literacy, they need learning opportunities that require them to transfer knowledge and skills to new situations in a safe, low-stakes environment and places where they can not only show what they know but also what they can do with what they know.

Richardson (2012) put it another way when he made the following request of teachers:

> Don't teach my child science; instead, teach my child how to learn science—or history, or math, or music. With as many resources as they have available to them

today (not to mention what they'll have tomorrow), kids had better know how. ("Transfer the Power," para. 4)

It is on this "knowing how" that the ILP attempts to focus, particularly when students reach the final assessment in a learning cycle. The "So what?" section pushes students to show what they learned and demonstrate its importance in an authentic way for an authentic audience. This is a lot to promise and a lot to ask of students and teachers. The ILP is a system that attempts to fulfill this promise.

Shifting the Responsibility of Learning

Because we designed the ILP to have as many opportunities for individualization as possible, by the end of each unit, students' plans are unique. As a result, the connections students make and insights they have are more likely to be their own. Even if students are reading a classic text, the ILP allows them to find their own way through it, discovering even well-worn themes through their own fresh lenses rather than trying to "guess what's in the teacher's head." We encourage you to share your own insights as a mentor, someone excited by the discovery that is happening for the student, which keeps the ownership of ideas in the students' hands. In this way, you become a fellow learner, remembering that students will answer questions differently than you would after the life experience you have had. Steven, an eleventh-grade student, explained his experience with the ILP this way: "This class was very hard work but yet I learned a whole lot because I got to study and learn my way. . . . You get to find out how you work and, most importantly, how you learn."

In addition to the skills and knowledge that students gain, they also think more broadly about education. Sadly, some students disregard education because they feel that it's antiquated or just a stepping-stone. The ILP really pushes students to examine how people learn and, in particular, how they learn best. One of the main things we learned is that the roles of students and teachers shouldn't be exclusive, and our hope is that the ILP will help students realize that they can be their own teachers. As a tenth grader, Bria, noted, the ILP is "not just going to one person who has all the answers; it's taking different answers and coming to a consensus to get to a central goal." This is a skill that students will use for the rest of their lives and that teachers can mentor along the way.

Students also become better at articulating and assessing their own skills and content knowledge, which will serve them well in the future. For students to make their own meaning, they need to experience learning that goes beyond the traditional classroom. The ILP requires the explicit teaching of more than content knowledge and skill acquisition. As Medina (2008) explained, "Babies are the model of how we learn—not by passive reaction to the environment but by active testing through observation, hypothesis, experiment, and conclusion" (p. 280). We're not meant to simply be receivers of knowledge. The ILP taps into this natural way of learning by encouraging students to remain active in the process, creating questions, consistently reflecting on their progress, and adjusting as needed.

Moving Forward

As a result of educational reform, experience, and reflection, we are currently on our tenth version of the ILP, but one thing hasn't changed: by the end of the process, students have discovered their own knowledge and are responsible for the skills they have developed. As you read through *Letting Go: How to Give Students Control over Their Learning in the English Classroom*, you'll find a variety of strategies with which to begin to let go of your prior conceptions of teaching, and, because the ILP is flexible, there are various options for how to begin, structure, and use the learning plan to best fit your students' needs. All parts are adaptable, but, because the ILP utilizes the core aspects of inquiry learning, we encourage you to read each part to see how they interact and intersect. When put together, the ILP has the potential to fulfill Richardson's (2012) hope for teaching and learning:

> Teachers need to be great at asking questions and astute at managing the different paths to learning that each child creates. They must guide students to pursue projects of value and help them connect their interests to the required standards. And they have to be participants and models in the learning process. ("Discover, Don't Deliver, the Curriculum," para. 6)

While this puts the focus on the changing role of the teacher, the ILP also attempts to push Chris Lehmann's proclamation for students: "It is their education, and it will be their world, and they deserve a voice in their own education" (TEDx Talks, 2010). We look forward to sharing our way of giving students the voice and challenge they deserve.

Explanation of Parts

Because the main purposes of this book are (a) to demonstrate that letting go is a rewarding experience and (b) to break down the strategies and processes that support a gradual release of responsibility to students, each part of the book begins with theory and our thinking behind the strategies before delving into a particular aspect of letting go. Throughout the book, we use student samples to demonstrate what these strategies look like. These parts and the chapters within them explain how you can use the strategies independently of one another or as part of the ILP. As a result, the process of letting go is scaffolded for both the student and the teacher. We also address issues and frustrations—or "pitfalls," as we call them—that you and your students may experience in an inquiry-based classroom and provide practical strategies for how to make sure you are all successful. Though we encourage you to move through the book in order, it is possible to utilize the strategies separately. Below is an overview of each of the book's parts, highlighting the goals of that section and some of the main strategies used to meet those goals.

Finally, while this book has ample excerpts of student work, we have also created an online appendix to share a few ILPs in their entirety and other supplemental materials. You can access the appendix at lettinggo-book.com with the password #ncteILP815.

Part I: Letting Go of the Pressure to Know Everything

Empowering Students to Discover

Somewhere along the way, teachers became synonymous with answers. In what many people call the "factory model," learning was more about the imparting of knowledge than the discovery of it. This ingrained attitude is what makes letting go of content—and putting it in the hands of students—so difficult for some teachers and even for some students. The "sage on the stage" model is revered in movies and television, especially in the English classroom. However, by letting students choose their own texts, ask their own questions, and discover their own answers, there is so much that can be gained—by students *and* their teachers. Since one of the tenets of this book is student choice, Part I elaborates on the importance of this theory and provides examples and reflections that show its power in the classroom.

Strategies for Beginning an Inquiry, Choosing Texts, and Developing Questions

While direct instruction still has a place in the classroom, we focus on strategies that empower students while ensuring that students are still learning what they need. This section zooms in on the beginning of the inquiry process by demonstrating how questions can stem from content, skills, or students' personal experiences. You will learn strategies to present this idea to students as well as to scaffold the choosing of texts and the creation of both GQs and EQs. To make meaning from questions, students must also examine texts that present a range of perspectives; however, the text selection process can be overwhelming for teachers and students. This section presents successful strategies such as giving text talks and using information portals created by librarians as well as strategies for working with reluctant readers through interest surveys and other resources.

This part also details pitfalls that students and teachers tend to encounter when attempting these strategies for the first time. You will learn how to recognize common missteps with question creation and the frustration and discomfort that comes when students are responsible for their own learning.

Part II: Letting Go of the "One-Size-Fits-All" Lesson Plan

Enabling Students to Learn How to Learn

Historically, teachers used a list of standards or other established skill sets to mold their units, and, while this approach does ensure that all students are walking away with a similar knowledge base, it also limits individualized, differentiated learning. Some students rush through or miss certain skills as they struggle to keep up with their peers, while others sit through repetitive lessons on skills they've already mastered. Part II explains why it's time to give up the search for the perfect lesson plan and allow students to practice skills that they most need to improve and that are most meaningful for them. It also explores how students can begin to take risks with their learning, practicing skills that might be new to them or pushing the limits of their previous understandings.

Strategies for Using Standards and Creating Activities

This part explains how to constructively introduce students to standards while also detailing strategies for continual work with them throughout the unit. You will learn strategies for examining the standards with students, such as defining verbs that reflect a skill and creating lists of possible products that would show successful mastery. You will then read about using diagnostics to help students choose standards, implementing student-created rubrics, and helping students synthesize these skills with their questions and texts. The strategies then shift to focus on activity design. During this process, students answer their questions, analyze their texts, and practice the standards. Using student examples, we show how activities progress over the course of the unit and when to have students complete activities as a whole class, with skill-focused groups, or as individuals.

Part II also explores some of the common pitfalls students and teachers might encounter when working with the standards for the first time. You will learn how to avoid the student isolation that can come with individualized work. This part also provides guidance for moments when students have misconceptions about the intention of a standard. Last, you will gain strategies for helping students design creative activities as they progress through the course.

Part III: Letting Go of the Grader

Entrusting Students with Charting Their Own Progress

As the experts in the room, teachers have always been at the center of assessment. This inquiry approach encourages you to shift some responsibility for assessment to students so they can become experts on their own learning. This might be difficult to imagine; however, if students never have the opportunity to articulate their own needs or assess their own progress, their learning is incomplete. To be independent learners, students need to move beyond being told how well they are doing. Instead, they need ample opportunities to set their own goals and create a plan for improvement. We illustrate how this shift in assessment responsibility can also increase each student's capacity for risk-taking and dealing with frustration. By using a mixture of formative, summative, self-, and peer assessment techniques, you can move students beyond "playing it safe" and push them toward independent learning and reflection.

Strategies for Assessment and Reflection

Using their knowledge of the standards and student-created rubrics, students begin to understand expectations and articulate their own abilities, successes, and learning needs. Additionally, they learn to work alongside their peers in order to give and receive feedback throughout the process. Part III walks you through teaching students how to assess their own work. Using skill-based flowcharts, rubrics, reflections, and conferences, students learn how to gauge their own progress. We also share techniques for helping you manage feedback and grading in this new paradigm. Part III further explains how formative assessment and feedback loops are an important part of the inquiry process, and describes how they lead up to summative assessments that provide the opportunity to demonstrate mastery of the skills students have been practicing. The reflective nature of self-assessment is guided by Kuhlthau's (2004) ISP (see Figure 2), which allows students to explain not only what and how they have learned a skill or concept but also the emotions that accompany the learning process. Last, this part of the book explores how a unit's final assessment can be authentic and turned over to the students in any classroom setting. Using the "So what?" final assessment, students share their learning beyond the classroom after creating a product that reflects their growth and understanding.

Furthermore, Part III explains how to help students when missteps occur while assessing their work. You will learn how to deal with student reluctance and how to help students recognize inaccuracies in their assessments. Finally, it details how to help students when they are inclined to focus more on the grade than on the process of learning and growth.

Part IV: Putting It All Together

Using the ILP So Students Can Take Control of Their Learning

Each of this book's parts discusses a different aspect of learning that can be handed over to the students. Once you become comfortable "letting go" of each of these areas, you can choose to let go of unit design as a whole, allowing students to truly craft their own learning. The final part guides you through one student's ILP. You will see the plan as a cohesive way to value students' interests and questions side by side with the standards for which they are responsible. In addition to the strategies provided throughout the book, Part IV explains how to scaffold this type of learning, working throughout a course to build students' comfort and understanding of inquiry.

Strategies for Using the ILP

When it comes to implementing the ILP, there are various ways to adapt it to fit the needs of a course. You will see (a) how the ILP may be used as a single unit for a course, and (b) how it can be used multiple times throughout a course, as you slowly scaffold the process from teacher-centered to student-centered learning. Two options for assessment of the ILP as a whole, both formative and summative, are explained, in addition to reinforcing the changing role of the teacher in an inquiry classroom and how the ILP helps the teacher to function in a facilitative role for the student's learning.

Guiding students through the creation of their own learning plan creates some unique challenges. You will learn how to help students manage their time as they work through the ILP as well as navigate the ILP itself, whether as a physical or an electronic document.

I

Letting Go of the Pressure to Know Everything

Empowering Students to Discover

How can teachers lead meaningful class discussions without everyone reading the same text? Don't students all need to explore the same themes when studying a novel? Aren't they losing a class bonding experience? Shouldn't every student read *The Great Gatsby*? Questions such as these are common reactions when we discuss the idea of giving students more curricular choice. But, before we reject this new and potentially uncomfortable approach, let's examine what is currently happening in some classrooms:

> When directed to discuss the color symbolism in *Gatsby*, a class of eleventh-grade students sits in a circle, facing one another. One student mentions that she noticed the colors associated with different aspects of Gatsby's party: the yellow dresses of a few guests and the blue gardens. Another student chimes in that those colors are also mentioned elsewhere in the book. The teacher asks what each of those colors might mean and whether the meaning seems to remain constant or change throughout the book. A third student raises her hand and responds with a well-supported argument about the purpose of colors as symbols for things like moral decay and wealth. "Brilliant!" the teacher responds and asks for additional evidence from the rest of the class. Looking around at the blank stares on at least half the students' faces, he prompts them to look back through the text for help. He tries calling on a student without his hand up, but he's greeted with a repetition of what other students have said. A few moments later, the first student raises her hand again and provides a quote and some analysis. When it comes time to write an essay at the conclusion of the unit a few weeks later, ten students write about the use of blue and yellow to represent wealth and moral decay in *The Great Gatsby*. Some even use the same quotes that their classmates mentioned in that discussion.

Although it is comforting to know that most students learn traditional symbols in a book that many English teachers deem essential, we also need to consider other important questions about what and how students are learning:

- Are all of my students equally motivated to work on this text?
- By focusing on select themes in this text, am I missing opportunities to see what my students find interesting?
- Are students able to connect with this discussion and find personal meaning in it?

These questions are just as important as our initial questions about shared texts and bonding experiences. In the discussion scenario above, students are learning from one another, but only a handful are really doing the work. They are essentially doing the thinking for the class, and, as a result, the preparation for everyone's future essays. Using these new questions to examine classroom dynamics also allows teachers to focus on individual student learning, inviting us to shift the expertise in the room from the teacher in order to value the experience and discovery of students.

Richardson (2012) explained this shift as he saw it and the "new" kind of teacher it would require:

> [W]hat our children really need are master learners with enough content expertise to help them discover the curriculum. The adults in the room have to be skilled and literate.... And they have to exhibit the dispositions that will sustain their learning: persistence, empathy, passion, sharing, collaboration, creativity, and curiosity. Most important, they have to be willing to learn with my children. ("Be a Master Learner," para. 14)

This willingness to learn along with children requires a vulnerability that isn't often associated with teaching. Teachers are seen as the "learned" and usually as the people who ask the questions and know the answers. Instead, what if we allowed students to pursue texts and topics that we may not know, ask their own questions, and discover their own answers? What can be gained from doing this, and is it worth what is lost?

Student Choice

Atwell (1987) has been inviting students to choose their own books for over thirty years. However, there's opportunity for choice beyond the selection of texts. Even if students are all reading the same text, you can encourage them to ask different questions, ones that have personal connections. When students initially create their course of inquiry, the focus is on finding a place where the curriculum and their interests meet. This is described by Maniotes as a "third space" that connects the first space of personal knowledge with the second space of the school curriculum so "students can construct new worldviews rather than having to take on the teacher's perspective or those mandated by the curriculum or textbook" (Kuhlthau, Maniotes, & Caspari, 2015, p. 27). The idea of third space pushes student interest into an equal arena with curricular focus and teacher knowledge, so it also may make some students uncomfortable. By the time students are in high school, we should not be surprised by the familiar refrain of "just tell me what to do" because that model is so ingrained by then. As McCombs (n.d.) pointed out, "The phenomenon of students taking less and less responsibility for their own learning is related to the fact that, in many school systems, students have progressively fewer opportunities to make choices as they proceed from elementary through secondary school" ("Reaching students through increased choices," para. 1). Students become less motivated to think for themselves and develop independence as learners and students; alternatively, the ILP gives students freedom and responsibility that motivates them to make discoveries that excite them.

Richardson (2012) has suggested that student choice is about building skills and habits of mind for the future and creating learners who are self-reliant:

> The emphasis shifts from content mastery to learning mastery. That means students have more ownership over their own learning, using their access to knowledge and teachers to create their own unique paths to the outcomes we, and they, deem important. ("Another Way," para. 2)

While it's true that all students in our opening scenario now know that the color yellow represents moral decay in *The Great Gatsby*, that has become a simple belief, one that's in every online study guide. If we want students to go beyond memorizing that tidbit, we need to see their thinking and their discoveries about the book instead. With the use of a "third space" and inquiry, students can uncover aspects of a text that might not even be on the teacher's radar. In turn, the students experience a sense of freedom. In an anonymous survey, when asked about choosing texts, one student responded:

> This really feels cool because if you didn't like a book in another class . . . guess what, you are going to have to suck it up and read that book . . . although it would be done in a month, you would just have no fun in that month of class. With this class, you get to choose what you want. AWESOME.

Extending the freedom from choosing texts to inviting students to ask their own questions is a great gift. As Martin-Kniep and Picone-Zocchia (2009) noted in their book *Changing the Way You Teach, Improving the Way Students Learn*, questions are important because:

> We discover the limitations of our understanding through the questions that we ask ourselves and those that others ask us. Questions enable us to define and

negotiate what we know and want to know, to test and expand the boundaries of our insights, and to differentiate our own thinking from that of others. Asking questions is the key to negotiating the differences between what is mundane and what is exquisite, what is busy work and what is transformative. Knowing what questions to ask and when to ask them gives us control over the knowledge we can negotiate. Teaching students to ask and ponder all kinds of questions, especially ones that can't be answered, can certainly produce better learners and thinkers than many of our current graduates. (p. 136)

Unfortunately, what Martin-Kniep and Picone-Zocchia (2009) saw in many classrooms were teachers asking "questions that they themselves can answer or whose answers are clearly available for the finding" (p. 137), such as the symbolism of the colors in *The Great Gatsby*. As they stated:

[Instead of] stimulating debate, probing assumptions, and delving into that gray area of no right and no wrong, classroom questions are much more likely to be focused on assessing or monitoring student comprehension, attention, or use of a strategy or process. In short, most teachers are far better at teaching students how to answer questions than how to pose good questions themselves. (p. 137)

This is an important distinction that we did not make in our own teaching prior to implementing the ILP. Using the themes and concepts with which we were comfortable, we guided students through a text instead of allowing them to discover and question it on their own. The latter approach is far more complex, requiring teachers to be (a) flexible, (b) willing to admit they don't know, and (c) practiced "questioners" who are comfortable with ambiguity. When students generate their own questions about a text or concept, you may experience discomfort, and then even more so if the student is studying something with which you are unfamiliar. However, this dynamic breaks down the "sage on the stage" paradigm and creates more of a community of learners.

Strategies for Beginning an Inquiry

How do we move into the "discomfort zone" and begin to shift away from rehearsed questions and answers? We put more responsibility in the hands of the students and recognize that they are capable of doing the kind of deep thinking that we aim to achieve. With the ILP model, we place more trust in the students to achieve that deep thinking through the study of something they choose to explore.

The first step in the process still falls to us, however. We need to determine where to begin, somewhere that grounds student inquiry with an educational need. Depending on the nature of the course, there are varying approaches to help students gain control of the content, and as the expert "learner" in the room, it is our responsibility to decide whether we want the learning process to begin with (a) texts, (b) desired skills, or (c) personal experience. Each starting point offers unique advantages, but they all inherently allow students to guide aspects of the learning process to fit their interests and/or needs. They also provide an invitation for students to initiate and invest in their paths of inquiry by serving as the context for the questions they establish. Where this begins will ultimately depend on what is at the core of the course and on your comfort level. The next few sections will provide examples to help you determine a point of entry for students, introducing strategies that explore the possibilities associated with each one. These strategies set the stage for doing inquiry work, and they should therefore be implemented prior to using the ILP.

Strategy: Starting with Content

Teaching specific books or concepts may be required in your curriculum. But even if you have the freedom to select texts and sculpt the curriculum, we recommend using common content the first time that students experience inquiry. This entry point helps to scaffold the process for students who might otherwise feel overwhelmed by the freedom that comes with self-directed learning. Starting with a common text or concept also provides an opportunity for differentiation while maintaining a foundation from which students can build. Providing students with the opportunity to determine their own points of departure helps them become more invested in the exploration of that content, even if it's not one that they might have chosen on their own.

Beginning with a common text might feel very similar to a traditional approach at first. For example, as students read the first chapter or two, they can note information they gather about elements such as themes, characters, rhetoric, or style; however, within the context of the ILP process, they do this with the intent to uncover something that provokes their sense of wonder, not simply to record encounters with traditional literary elements. Note-taking guides like Beers and Probst's (2012) "signposts" or Kittle's (2012) "response to quotations" can help students keep track of information from a text, and later guide them to develop questions. You can also guide students with broad questions like "What are the emerging themes?," "What is the writing style?," or "Are there any historical or social allusions?"

When a sophomore class read Alexandra Robbins's *The Geeks Shall Inherit the Earth*, they tackled Chapter 1 with the following prompts:

- How does Robbins organize the chapter? Does this help your understanding of the content or is it distracting or confusing?

- Choose one quote from the chapter that you believe exemplifies the main idea of the chapter. Incorporate the quote into an analytical paragraph and explain how this quote relates to the overall chapter.

- Record any questions you may have as you read.

This helped the students to begin thinking about the decisions that the author made and the purpose of the text while considering their own experience and insight. It also scaffolded the reading process (while going beyond checking for reading comprehension) and modeled one way to approach texts in the future. Student responses were shared in small inquiry groups and in large class discussions. Sharing their responses also provided forums for students to develop any questions that might be occurring to them already.

Another option for starting with content involves slightly more choice when it comes to a text, but it may still be rooted in a single theme or concept determined by the teacher. For example, in an honors sophomore class, students studying creativity worked from texts they found in order to decide a personal direction for the common topic. Jillian, a tenth-grade student in Cathy's class, showed us her thought process while noting interesting quotes from *Creating*

Minds: An Anatomy of Creativity Seen through the Lives of Freud, Einstein, Picasso, Stravinsky, Eliot, Graham, and Gandhi by Howard Gardner (see Figure 3). In the featured section, she blended self-selected quotes from the text (some by Einstein and some by Gardner) with her own ideas.

p.88 "Young Einstein exhibited another revealing tendency: he posed gritty questions and then pondered them at length."
He wondered things like "would this ever happen?" and "what would happen if…?" and "what would it be like if…?"
"This proclivity for imagining and pondering puzzles persisted."

Einstein wondered about what had caused him to explore these areas and pose these questions. He self-reflected, "The reason, I think, is that a normal adult never stops to think about problems of space and time. These are things which he has thought of as a child. But my intellectual development was retarded…" Einstein hypothesized that his slow development allowed him to have his mind dwell in the imaginative child stages, therefore he could "go deeper" into the things that struck his interest.

This leads to another question:
- Are people more creative as children than they are as adults?

And these questions stem from it:
- Should the minds of children be used in our modern world of progress alongside those of adults?
   - Should children be placed in more chief positions?
      - If we did this, and took children out of schools to do work specified to their individual creative power, what would result?
- Can children be more beneficial than we think as far as contributing to the world, by means of using their creativity?

Evidential answers: Einstein seemed to think so. "He had once declared that we know all the physics we will ever need to know by the age of three."

….Words in that excerpt ("The reason, I think, is that a normal adult never stops to think about problems of space and time. These are things which he has thought of as a child. But my intellectual development was retarded…") triggered me to make that question. It might be "a normal adult never stops to think" because it begins to make me think, well, obviously adults are thinking, but are we thinking about the wrong things? We're not *really* thinking? And then they went on to say that Einstein thought of these things as a child…and never stopped thinking of them as an adult. Clearly, Einstein thought about intelligent things as an adult, and if he thought about them as a child, and he's saying they are things that all children think of, then it leads me to think that we should think more like children in our adult years.
This poses another question:
- Is it even *possible* for adults to think more like children, or for children to continue to think in the way that they do their entire lives?
   - Is there a way to avoid entering the mainstream?
Because, according to Einstein, children's thought processes are significantly important.

FIGURE 3. Student notes on *Creating Minds*.

Clearly, these quotes sparked many questions for her. And, while Jillian hadn't decided on a specific question for her inquiry yet, she was invested in the topic of creativity because she was able to think about aspects of it that were interesting to her. Her classmates, although focusing on the same topic, were doing some preliminary thinking around creativity, such as the benefits of restricted creativity and creativity's origins. They were equally invested in those ideas because they came to them on their own. Had Cathy simply dictated, "We're all going to study the benefits of creativity," much like the teacher who prompted students to explore color symbolism in *The Great Gatsby*, some of the students might have been intrigued. But even the students most naturally aligned with the teacher's curiosity might not have taken ownership of or shown the enthusiasm for a topic that Jillian did.

Strategy: Starting with Skills

For courses that are centered more on skills, such as public speaking and creative writing, you can designate specific skills as a beginning point for student inquiry. Typically, reading, writing, and speaking/listening skills are at the core of any English class, and diagnostic assessments or previous work can help teachers get a pulse on students' abilities in those core areas. They serve as a baseline to inform both the teacher and the students of strengths and weaknesses, and they can help us to identify gaps in understanding. Those knowledge gaps can then become the basis of exploration.

In Meg's Honors Imaginative Process course, one with an advanced creative writing curriculum, students began a screenplay unit by first watching the opening scene from the pilot episode of the show *Lost* (Abrams & Lindelof, 2004). After watching the clip a few times and taking notes, students made their first attempt at re-creating the screenplay for the scene, either alone or with a partner. As with many diagnostics, this exercise was a struggle for some students since they had not been exposed to this mode of writing before, but this confusion and frustration established a lack of skills. After attempting writing on their own, students then read the published script, comparing their work to the professional script. To reflect on the exercise, students were asked the following questions:

- How is your script different from the actual one? Why are they different?
- What did you leave out that you now realize was important?
- Based on what you watched, would you have added anything to the published script to make elements clearer to a reader (rather than a viewer)?

From here, students established the skills and knowledge they needed in order to explore the art of screenplay writing and create scripts of their own.

Strategy: Starting with Personal Experience

You can also begin with student interests, an approach that puts value on students' passions over content and skills. One way to help uncover student interests is to use student surveys, like those of Cushman (2010). In *Fires in the Mind: What Kids Can Tell Us about Motivation and Mastery,* she asked teachers and students to reflect on learning experiences to discover what makes them pursue something even when they know it is difficult. As she observed, "Something they valued . . . always gave meaning and momentum to those first steps into learning" (Cushman, 2010, p. 28). By studying their responses to questions about interests and activities, we can look "for a pattern of learning that can guide us" (p. 28) as we help students begin their inquiry.

Through a survey variation of Cushman's (2010) "Many Interests, Many Strengths" discussion prompts, Mike, an eleventh-grade student with in-class support, revealed that he wanted to learn more about the ocean. The survey itself provided a checklist with the prompt, "Which of the above areas do you wish you could learn more about?" The choices included Cushman's suggested topics, such as sports and physical challenges, arts, logic puzzles, and nature. It also included an "other" category for students to write in their own topics. That's where Mike decided to make his interest in "nature" more specific by writing in "the ocean." He wrote, "I have always loved the ocean and I try to know much about it since most of the sports I do involve the water and/or ocean." He revealed in another response that he had been bodyboarding since he was four.

As Cushman (2010) suggested, Mike's survey responses provided an opportunity for discussion and teacher–student connection. After reading Mike's answers, his teacher, Cathy, conferenced with him to ask questions like, "What do you already know about the ocean?" and "What do you find most interesting about it?" With these prompts, he could start to pinpoint what he loved—the power and force of waves, the ocean's unpredictability, and how he felt a part of it when he was on his surfboard. Cathy took notes during that brief getting-to-know-you conference, and, by the end, she handed him a record of his unique reflections on nature, the ocean, and his connection to it. She suggested that he focus his reading on those elements.

Mike used his personal interests and experience as a lens for approaching texts during the first unit. As the class studied American Romanticism and read common works by writers like Emerson, Whitman, and Dickinson, Mike focused on man's connection to nature and his occasional helplessness against its power. Other students focused on topics such as independence and ingenuity, social imbalances, collaboration, and coexistence. Though all students were analyzing and interpreting the same texts, they used a personal connection to build their inquiry, which left a more lasting impression.

Another strategy for establishing and pursuing student interests is freewriting. In one sophomore class, each student kept a blog on which they could write about whatever they were thinking, as long as it was school appropriate. Students wrote about anything from reactions to classical music scores to last night's gymnastics workout to difficulties with a math class. At the end of each blog post, students were encouraged to pose a question—for themselves and their peers—that required further exploration. The questions became fodder for their unit questions and, eventually, for their text studies. For example, Cassandra, who was reflecting on media and technology's influence on her and her peers, ultimately asked, "How much can we independently impact our lives?" Another student blogged about some peers who complained that they couldn't remember information for another class even though they could easily gossip about who was wearing what and dating whom. She wanted to know why some information is memorable and other information slips away. Both of these students used the questions they were struggling with to frame their personal inquiries.

Of all the inquiry starting points outlined in this chapter, personal connection leads to the most individualization because students begin with their own unique experiences. Whether prompted by teacher conferences, interest surveys, or freewriting, students can go on to create questions or find texts that fit their individual learning needs.

Pitfall: When Students Are Uneasy with the Responsibility of Choice from the Outset

To prepare students for the freedom that inquiry offers, try an inquiry experience on a smaller scale. For example, in an American Literature course, Heather and Cathy began a discussion with a deceptively simple question: "What is a text?" This question is deceptive because most students thought the answer was concrete and immediate until we started to answer as a group (see Figure 4).

Though most students began with the dictionary definition, through discussion, comparison, questioning, and debate, they realized the idea that at first seemed clear cut was open to possibility, based on culture, perspective, and their own personal ideas of communication. They ended their discussion in a very different place than they started; everyone used their experiences to answer the question, and they all learned from one another. We remained guides, letting the students hash out ideas and come to conclusions but not necessarily consensus.

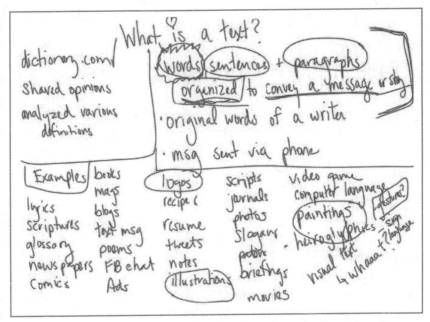

FIGURE 4. "What is a text?" screen capture from class discussion. Reproduced from "Inquiry Learning: The Starting Point," by M. Donhauser, H. Hersey, C. Stutzman, and M. Zane, 2014b, *School Library Monthly* (an imprint of ABC-CLIO), *31*(2), p. 9. CC BY-NC-SA.

This question did two important things to prepare students for the responsibility that comes with inquiry, as well as with the freedom of choice: (1) it broadened their conception of the word *text* and (2) it provided a great model for discussing an idea that is not as simple as they first imagined. They got to hear the class working out an inquiry, which allowed them to see other approaches to answering the question. They also experienced the types of questions that we would be asking them as they started their own inquiries.

Strategies for Choosing Texts

Although some students may begin their inquiries with common, teacher-selected texts, others will need to select their own to help them explore the topics from their personal experience or help them practice their chosen skills. In fact, having students choose their own texts might be a familiar step for many English teachers, who follow in the footsteps of practitioners like Kittle (2012) and Atwell (1987). Regardless of whether you choose to start with a text, skill, or personal interest, students can list their different texts and resources in the first part of the ILP, fittingly called "What I will read" (see Figure 5).

If we think of texts as being either core or supplemental, we allow for various approaches to having students make decisions about what texts they will choose. *Core texts* are at the center of inquiry and serve to help answer students' questions. These are the texts that many teachers in traditional settings would have built their units around. *Supplemental texts* cover a variety of purposes, such as supporting students' inquiry and helping them to master skills. As students progress through a unit and notice gaps in their knowledge and skills, they can choose supplemental texts to support their unique learning needs. These could include anything from author biographies, to timelines for historical context, to literary criticism about a major text, to explanations of concepts on Wikipe-

What I Will Read
List the core materials below.
List resources below that will aid your inquiry.

FIGURE 5. "What I will read" section of the ILP.

dia. (See Figure 61 in Part IV of this book for an example of how this looks in an ILP.) If your curriculum already has core texts chosen, supplementary texts are an option to allow choice and have students find their own resources and make connections during reading. Requiring supplementary texts encourages students to be active readers, always on the lookout for places to dig for more.

Though choice of supplemental texts is an excellent introduction to "letting go," it is really the choice of core texts that allows students to truly connect to their learning. Core texts are studied for both content and style, so allowing choice at this stage gives you a way to differentiate for students' ability levels. As the teacher, you should first decide what requirements you want for your students' texts that will help them to answer their EQs—choice of text can run the gamut of a single article to an entire unit of student-selected texts. Figure 6 shows how Meg instructed students to choose certain types of texts required by the curriculum. Everyone used *Macbeth* as a core text, but each student was required to choose two other core texts to study, ensuring a variety of lenses through which students viewed the play. For example, students needed to read a bit of *Macbeth* before they could decide on a poem that addressed the same themes. Additionally, students chose supplemental texts throughout the process as their needs arose. Below, you will find several strategies for helping students choose their own texts.

What I Will Read
List the core materials below.   •   Full class text: *Macbeth*   •   Choice poem: •   Choice non-fiction: List resources below that will aid your inquiry.

FIGURE 6. "What I will read" from the ILP (with specific text selection requirements).

Strategy: Getting Recommendations from Others

When students are choosing texts, you can design the experience to allow for a lot or a little freedom. Students can choose a core text from a list of pre-approved books that fulfill a certain educational need, but this might lead students to simply pick a title they have heard of before and not to explore any other options. This is where text talks and your school's teacher-librarians become invaluable resources. In *text talks*, librarians or teachers share texts that relate to the students' needs for the unit. They are similar to book talks, but using the word *text* opens up the selection to other types of creations, including films, podcasts, and art. The selected text could be derived from curricular needs (like literary eras in an American Literature class) or based on student interests. Books can be selected by the librarian or teacher ahead of time based on EQs or areas of study. When introducing a book, the "text talker" can give students a glimpse of the characters, setting, conflict, and overall nature of the book by either reading a section, providing a "book trailer," showing a video clip of an author interview, or asking provocative questions. Text talks can be done in the classroom or in the library and collaboratively with librarians, teachers, and even students. By including students, these talks become a way to discuss literacy and favorite texts or authors as a class.

While student text talks can become a routine part of your class, they are not the only option for peer text recommendations. Our students often share all aspects of their work with one another in small groups or through Google Drive, a web application that allows for the storage and sharing of documents such as their ILPs. Once they have seen or heard what other students are studying, they may choose to collaborate on a text that would suit their own inquiry. Access to one another's text choices helps to increase students' collaboration skills and build class culture. This opens students up to the interests of their classmates, which serves to help them discover common interests or create new ones, and simply encourages them to get to know one another better on their way to becoming a community of learners.

Strategy: Allowing Time to Browse

Time is precious in the classroom, and thinking involves time. These two concepts often butt heads in school; however, if you want students to make thoughtful choices, they need time to browse. Because text talks and recommendations narrow what students can choose from, they do not teach students the skills required to narrow and evaluate choices on their own. Allowing time to casually search for texts gives students space to learn this important skill. One way to encourage more freedom in the search but still set parameters is for teacher-librarians to create project guides and learning portals to help with the exploration phase and text selection. LibGuides are content management systems often used in libraries; the LibGuide shown in Figure 7 categorizes resources for students in an American Literature class so that they can narrow and broaden their text searches by literary awards, eras, or writers, among other topics.

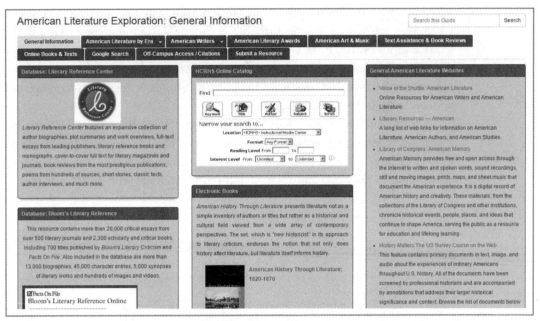

FIGURE 7. LibGuide for American literature. Reproduced with permission from Marci Zane.

Early in the inquiry process, students should be given ample time to browse the information available to them in the guides because, if we want students to invest in the resources we present, we need to give them time to explore them. This is also true for providing browsing time in the library. When browsing for information is assigned for homework, we assume that students have the necessary skills and time to be successful. However, by providing time to seek with experts in the room, we show the value in this part of the process and are available to guide students through these sometimes unfamiliar and daunting physical and digital environments.

Strategy: Inquiry Logs

Inquiry logs are a tool to help keep students organized as they begin searching for texts, allowing them to record texts they might want to use later in the unit. You could also use these logs to introduce students to key texts or themes from categories such as time period or genre to ensure students are choosing texts that relate to a unit's overall theme or purpose. For example, in Meg's British Literature course, in which units are organized by time period, students need an overview of what was happening at the time in order to choose texts. During a Renaissance and Reformation unit, students are provided a partially complet-ed inquiry log with a few resources to get them started (e.g., one of the Crash Course series on YouTube; Green & Green, n.d.), an overview of the time period from a literary anthology, and one of Shakespeare's sonnets as an example of lit-erature from the period (as shown in Figure 8). Students then find the remaining sources to help them begin their inquiry.

Another use for inquiry logs is on planned days in the school's library. For example, when Cathy spends a class period in the library with her students, after they have selected their core texts, and usually after they have developed their initial inquiry questions, she will provide students with additional time to

INQUIRY LOG

Use this log to record your thoughts as you read. You can write directly on this sheet, on a separate sheet of paper, or you can access this page on Google Drive.

	Citation: Provide author, title, and/or quote. For a long section, you can just write down the first few words and the last few words. Make sure you record enough so that you'll know what to go back to.	Why is this passage interesting or useful? This can be a personal note, a brief comment, or a question.	Explore further.	Don't explore further.
1	"Crash Course: Renaissance" https://www.youtube.com/watch?v=Vufb a_ZcoR0			
2	"The Early Modern Period: At a Glance"			
3	Shakespeare's Sonnet 116			
4				
5				

FIGURE 8. Sample inquiry log. Adapted from *Guided Inquiry Design: A Framework for Inquiry in Your School* (Figure 6.3), by C. C. Kuhlthau, L. K. Maniotes, and A. K. Caspari, 2012, Santa Barbara, CA: Libraries Unlimited. Adapted with permission.

browse for shorter works of poetry or short stories in databases, on the web, or in hard-copy collections. As they browse, she asks students to read about the texts or begin reading the text itself. If they are inclined to keep reading because the text has piqued their interest, she asks them to list the source in their inquiry logs. She gives her students a blank version of the template shown in Figure 8. Even if students haven't finished reading the text yet, they are encouraged to write initial thoughts about its role in their inquiry. She also asks them to write down up to ten texts, even though they only need four for the purpose of the unit. By doing so, students have a list of many potential resources for their explorations, and, no matter where their thinking takes them, they have several resources to look to for guidance.

In the preceding examples, inquiry logs are used to (a) give an overview of the unit's focus, which then branches into an EQ, or (b) track core or supplementary texts that help students answer their EQs. However, the flexibility that inquiry logs offer can lead to many other uses.

Strategy: Conferring with Teachers and Librarians

Conferring is another strategy for assisting students as they search for great sources and build the skills to do so in other instances. Just as librarians conduct reference interviews to support patrons, conferencing allows teachers and librarians to uncover thoughts that may have gone unsaid and to probe further where students may not have. Once students start to choose texts with guidance, they begin to understand their needs and the types of questions that can help to uncover them. This ability will serve them well as they move into a world that relies less on knowledge and more on finding information, connecting ideas, and building on them—but it all starts with teachers finding room for student choice in their curricula.

For a digital way to aid students in their search for texts, you can create a "text assistance request form" (see Figure 9). Two simple questions—"What do you need?" and "What have you tried already?"—provide a clear picture of where student research skills might be lacking. If students hit a stumbling block, this form can uncover their feelings and enable you to intervene before these students reach an unproductive level of frustration.

"Text" Assistance Request Form

Need help finding a text? Tell us what you've tried and what you need, and we'll try to help you!

* Required

Name *

[   ]

What have you tried so far in your search for a text? (databases, web searches, etc.) *

[   ]

What type of text do you need? Be as specific as possible about what you are looking for. *

[   ]

[Submit]

Never submit passwords through Google Forms.

FIGURE 9. Text assistance request form.

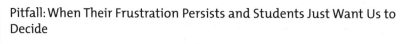

Pitfall: When Their Frustration Persists and Students Just Want Us to Decide

Usually, as an inquiry unit progresses, students become more comfortable with the freedom of choice. However, for some, the confusion and discomfort of uncertainty continues. For example, when asked what they would change about the freedom to choose their own texts and create their own questions, some American literature students expressed a longing for a more traditional setup:

I think maybe analyzing popular texts from different lit eras together as a class can help us understand what you expect as a teacher and work on our analytical skills in general. (We all know that synthesis papers never go away in college!)

I feel like the class was more complicated [than] it should have been. There's no definite answer and we spent so much time looking for sources.

When faced with these reactions from students, it can be easy to get frustrated as well and fall back on what's comfortable. However, doing so conveys to students that their ability to discover, to persevere, and to challenge themselves is not as important as getting through material quickly and easily. It also demonstrates that there will be someone to feed them answers when finding them on their own is challenging—something that rarely happens in life. Instead, we need to persevere, too. We need to show students that we understand their frustrations and that we want to help them work through those rough patches. At the same time, we also don't want to bend so much that the integrity of the inquiry process is lost. We want to make sure they understand that we will not tell them what to do and we will not give them the answers, but we will work with them to figure out some new strategies to better support them. In fact, we often share the research behind our pedagogy with students, so they understand how we ground our assumptions about learning. Here are a few techniques we found helpful:

- *Validation*—We reassure them by saying, "It makes sense that you're confused or frustrated" or "This is a difficult process." We refer back to Kuhlthau's (2004) ISP (see Figure 2) to remind them that research has normalized the uncertainty, confusion, frustration, and doubt of the early stages of inquiry as well as the good feelings such as clarity and confidence if they can work through it.

- *Conferences*—Some concerns cannot be addressed through written comments. If students are really frustrated, we can use questions to pinpoint why and ask them to show where in the process that frustration is occurring. Conferences not only solve immediate problems, but they also model for students the problem-solving process so that, next time, the students will have viable strategies.

- *Peer mentors*—Getting to know students' strengths allows us to pair them with students who need support in this area.

- *Full-class instruction*—If most students are struggling, take time for a mini-lesson on strategies such as questioning or searching for texts. A quick reminder of browsing techniques can spark ideas for students.

3

Strategies for Developing Questions

As Burke (2010) pointed out in his book *What's the Big Idea?*, Socrates used questions to structure learning, so this concept isn't new; however, as he also affirmed, a test-heavy culture has moved teaching away from using big questions (pp. 1–2). This is unfortunate because research by Marzano, Pickering, and Pollock (2001) has revealed that high-level questions are particularly effective when used "before a learning experience to establish a 'mental set' with which students process the learning experience" (qtd. in Burke, 2010, p. 2). It can be even more effective when students create these questions themselves. As a result, it's important for students to understand that there are different types and levels of questions—that questions can build upon each other and lead to more questions. Repeated practice creating and modifying questions builds "in our students the mental acuity and fluency necessary to succeed in school and at work, as well as to achieve a sense of purpose in their personal lives" (Burke, 2010, p. 10). Practice with questions also helps students to develop a skill that will transfer from subject to subject and beyond school. As one group of senior English students explained, questions serve "as an engine to creating a voice and identity for each individual student." Though there are oodles of resources that focus on improving a teacher's ability to ask good questions (Burke, 2010; McTighe & Wiggins, 2013; Wilhelm, 2007), our emphasis is on helping students unlock their own ability to develop questions.

When using the ILP, students list their inquiry questions for the unit in the "What I will learn" section (see Figure 10). These questions can stem from the three building blocks of the ILP: content, skills, or personal experience. However, each of the strategies discussed in the following sections can be used without the ILP to help students develop their own questions.

What I Will Learn
Please list your essential and guiding questions that you plan on pursuing this unit.

FIGURE 10. "What I will learn—Questions" from the ILP. Adapted from "The Inquiry Learning Plan: Creating Engaging Questions," by M. Donhauser, H. Hersey, C. Stutzman, and M. Zane, 2015a, *School Library Monthly* (an imprint of ABC-CLIO), *31*(3), p. 8. CC BY-NC-SA.

Strategy: Defining and Introducing EQs

Before students begin creating questions to guide their inquiry, we want them to understand how questions function and how asking an effective question will impact the type of information they will be seeking. Therefore, it's important to discuss sample questions, asking what words such as *how* and *why* mean. What kind of information do they produce? How might you search for information differently when asking an "is" question versus a "why" question? This analysis of language leads to a discussion about which words make a question more compelling, which is why we spend time differentiating between question types like "essential" and "guiding" questions (herein, EQs and GQs). Martin-Kniep and Picone-Zocchia (2009) defined them in this way: "*Essential* questions are universal questions that have no definitive answer. . . . *Guiding* questions, distinctly different from essential questions, are both specific and answerable" (pp. 141–42).

These discussions establish a common vocabulary with which to talk about and assess questions. Both of these question types are crucial to the inquiry process, and each serves a unique purpose. EQs, a part of Wiggins and McTighe's (2005) "backward design" model, are the umbrella or overarching questions of the unit. Traditionally, teachers have developed EQs that they feel are necessary for their courses. But this approach is too narrow. Since Wiggins and McTighe (2005) encouraged us to see EQs as "important questions that recur throughout all our lives" (p. 108), it is crucial to let students create questions that will be important to them. For example, Nolan, a student in an Honors British Literature class, developed the question "Are we all damned?" This question, inspired by texts like *A Clockwork Orange* and *The Satanic Verses* (see Figure 11), doesn't have a definitive answer. It needs to be revisited occasionally as someone moves through different experiences and interacts with new sources of information.

What I Will Read
Each unit will explore five texts from the time period. One of these texts must be a long text, meaning it is 150 pages or longer. The remaining texts can be any genre, but remember that they must be by a British writer and from the assigned time period. 1.   A Clockwork Orange by Anthony Burgess 2.   The Satanic Verses by Salman Rushdie 3.   Infant Innocence by A.E. Houseman 4.   Burial of the Dead by T.S. Eliot 5.   Ash-Wednesday by T.S. Eliot During your exploration, you must also use additional resources to help you explore the time period, the authors, and/or the texts. These can be pieces of literary criticism, author bios, essays about the literary movements, etc. List those additional resources below. 1.   http://www.tandfonline.com/doi/abs/10.1080/08957690309598481#.UZ4LYaK-IIE 2.   The Bible

FIGURE 11. "What I will read" from Nolan's ILP.

Strategy: Defining and Introducing GQs

Whereas EQs are philosophical, GQs are more practical in nature. GQs will help students answer their EQs and act as the building blocks of their inquiries because they often require more specific information. Students may develop only one or two EQs for a unit, but they will have many GQs, inspired by content, skills, or personal experiences.

When we introduce GQs to our students, we turn back to Martin-Kniep and Picone-Zocchia (2009) and their explanation of divergent and convergent questions:

> Questions can . . . be classified according to their open-endedness. *Convergent* questions focus on a correct response and reflect given or remembered information. . . . *Divergent* questions are more demanding of the student's thought process and may call for several plausible or correct responses. (pp. 140–41)

Most of the GQs that students ask will fall under the definition of convergent questions and will help students focus on a specific, supported response. This is not to say that convergent questions are simple; they are answered through a thought process that requires a narrowing of ideas and complex thinking. For example, Nolan, the British literature student from the previous section on EQs, developed the question "Are we all damned?" and he then created GQs for his texts that helped to answer his overarching EQ:

- Is the main character religious?
- Why does the main character do bad things?
- Is the main character still a protagonist if he does bad things?
- Are the characters cursed at birth to sin?

These questions are text-based and, therefore, a specific answer emerges from the text, but they still require complex thinking and evidence. Additionally, his first question could have a "yes" or "no" answer, which may then inspire more questions.

Divergent questions are similar to EQs in that they are big, universal questions that require reading, research, experience, and a student's speculation to justify a response. Different or alternative answers are possible, and often no one answer is right. Though most of the GQs from our students are convergent, sometimes students' EQs are so broad that they may need to use some larger, divergent questions as their GQs. For example, Nolan felt he needed to consider the following GQs when attempting to answer his EQ "Are we all damned?":

- Why do we choose to not conform?
- What does it mean to be good/evil?
- Is there really pure good and pure evil?
- Does society choose what is good, or has it been chosen by elements beyond our control?
- Are we destined to sin?
- Do we all come from the same god?

While any of these questions could also serve as an EQ, given their open nature, Nolan was most invested in the question about damnation; these questions may not have specific answers, but his teacher, Meg, didn't want to impede his process by forcing all of his GQs to be convergent. He needed to go through this process to develop a complex, well-rounded response to his initial EQ. Last, it is important for students to understand that their GQs should be varied in format and must include both comprehension questions and questions that require critical thinking and close-reading skills in order to reach a comprehensive and defensible answer.

Strategy: Using a Teacher-Created EQ to Generate Individual GQs

Some teachers work with students who may not be ready to start an inquiry from scratch. Other teachers may need to study specific content and do not have the freedom to allow students to choose their own questions. For these instances, giving an EQ that is large enough to encompass many interests is a great strategy. For example, in the first unit of Meg's Honors Imaginative Process class, the course curriculum dictated that students explore the concept of art; therefore, she gave the class an overarching EQ: "What is art?" After reading various teacher- and student-chosen introductory texts, students developed their own GQs in order to personalize their learning. The following questions were from the Spring 2014 class:

- How do you "art"?

- What is an efficient way to target and capture a particular audience?

- What is the correct way to utilize the "writing process" in order to create art?

These three questions encouraged students to think about the skills necessary to create art. They asked themselves what they needed to be able to do to create art. From this discussion, they decided to focus on poetry and created the following questions, which would address both their reading and writing skills:

- What is the relationship between the author and the audience?

- What literary devices are effective in poetry and how can they be incorporated in yours?

- What types of words/phrases keep you interested?

- How have your personal experiences shaped the connotative meanings? What are the connotative/denotative meanings?

- How does the author use punctuation?

- What specific words allow the reader to know the tone of the poem?

- How do spaces/line breaks affect the meaning of the poem?

- How does the structure/language of the poem relate to its message?

- What figurative language is used to add imagery to the poem?

- What's the poem's rhyme scheme? Meter?

These questions get to the fine details of poetry writing and are reminiscent of typical questions we might give a student when analyzing poetry. However, because these questions were developed based on what the students saw as their learning needs, they held more weight in their learning process. One student, Lizzie, reflected:

> I was most interested in learning about "what is creativity?" The reason this question interested me so much was because a writer has to be creative in order to be successful. There [are] so many writers and standing out is hard. As we read *Alice in Wonderland*, this question really sparked more and more curiosity. Also reading [supplementary texts] about what is art and *duende* helped me become interested as well. My . . . poem really helped me bring out my creativity and answer my essential question.

Lizzie realized the struggle an author has in creating a unique voice, and, as a result, explored texts that would help her bring *duende,* or the "soul" of art, into her poetry. She studied what a successful writer had done and applied that to her own work, challenging her own creativity.

Strategy: Using GQs to Establish an EQ

In the next unit, which focused on short story writing, students approached question development in a different way. First, they developed GQs based on the writing skills they needed for that genre (e.g., "What is essential to a short story?" and "Is it better to know everything that is going to happen before you begin to write the story or should you just let it unfold?"). These skill-based GQs were used to create EQs like Shea's: "Does fiction shape or reflect reality?" This question is philosophical and broad and requires close study of an author's craft. Shea explained how he developed this question:

> The question came from talking with a friend about Jack Kerouac and how he wrote about his actual life. So, in his case, he wrote from the reflection of his own reality. However, I myself have experienced times where fiction has changed my perspective. And so what I wanted to find was proof that the best [stories] not only were a reflection of the author's reality, but was able to shape the reader's reality as well by putting them into the shoes of someone totally different than themselves. Which could not be accomplished by anything other than a great book.

In this case, GQs that were grounded in skills and craft were necessary for this course, but they can also be more closely tied to the content or a personal connection. This will lead to more thematic EQs. For example, in a later unit of the same course, Noah, a senior, asked the GQs "How did many different religions come about and not just one?" and "What are the different types of religion?" to ultimately develop the EQ "What would life be like without religion?" These students used very different GQs to arrive at their EQs. A personal GQ is not only important for class but also shows students how asking questions leads to better understanding in all aspects of life. Questions aren't barriers to be answered but opportunities to build on.

Pitfall: When Students Bite Off More Than They Can Chew

Of course, we want our students to achieve as much as possible, but what happens when they overextend themselves on a question that is too complex for the time or resources they have? Bria, a senior in an honors writing class who had already used the ILP in her sophomore year, began planning for her unit by developing these three questions:

- What is the common thread that ties together the narratives of black women?
- How does ignoring the negative side of reality impact one's perception of the present?
- Where does my story fit in?

As a young black woman, she wanted to know how her own story related to the stories of others, including Zora Neale Hurston and Janet Mock. She had started brainstorming for her unit by reading Hurston's essay "How It Feels to Be Colored Me," and as a result was also wondering how ignorance of black women's history impacted contemporary women. She felt passionately about each question, but all three could be the study of an individual unit. Since this student was overwhelmed by exploring so many avenues in a limited amount of time, Meg sat down with her to discuss what it was about each question that she felt was important. Meg could see a connection among the three, but, instead of telling Bria, she wanted her to make her own connections. Meg let natural curiosity guide the conversation, asking questions like, "Do you think there is a common theme to your life story?" and "Do you think all black women might relate?" Bria then realized she could study stories and compare them to her own. From there, Meg asked, "If everybody has a story, how come you chose Hurston and Mock? Why did you choose them?" That's when the lightbulb went off: Bria realized she truly wanted to learn about why some voices have an impact and if her own could as well; in the end, she created the question "How do we assign value to a story?" as her question for the unit. When a student is trying to answer a question that requires too much time or information, you can step in to ask about the common threads or what means the most to the student as a learner. If we lead students too much, the questions become ours, not theirs. Accordingly, we try to maintain a curious learning stance despite our excitement about our own knowledge.

Strategy: Question Lenses

Though creating EQs and GQs is a crucial early step of the ILP, some students will need more practice creating questions in general. One strategy for question development that allows students to "try on" different questions is the use of lenses. The following activity was adapted from Valenza's (2004) "Question Brainstormer." Students look at two topics of interest through five different lenses with examples of each (see Figure 12). After students complete this activity, we ask them two questions about their questions (yes, very meta!):

1. Which question is best in terms of critical thinking?
2. Which question will help you best in terms of learning about your topic?

Interrogating their questions in this way helps students better understand how questions work. Without this second step, they might just choose a question haphazardly; however, by selecting and even ranking the possibilities, students not only find interesting questions but they also begin to see that not all questions are equal.

Strategy: Teaching Question Types

If you are familiar with Bloom's (1956) taxonomy, you can adapt its language for an additional strategy to guide students through question creation. The following question types (in Figure 13), adapted from "Yo Socrates! Amend This!" (Eisen, 2007) and Bloom's taxonomy, use the story of the "Three Little Pigs" to provide examples. Like the question lenses strategy, this exercise pushes students to test out different question types and makes explicit the difference between lower- and higher-order questions.

Regardless of their beginning point, students can work in small groups on the challenge of developing a question for each type outlined in Figure 13. A group from the sophomore class that was studying *The Geeks Shall Inherit the Earth* came up with the following questions using this strategy:

- KNOWLEDGE: Which clique is standard/normal for the general public, when most of these students grew up at the same time?
- OPEN-ENDED: How would the school in *Geeks* be different if band geeks were popular and the popular groups were nerds?

list continued on p. 49

Question Lens and Examples	Topic #1	Topic #2
Which one? Purpose: Collect information to make an informed choice. Topic: Fantasy writing Example: Which author had the biggest impact on fantasy writing?		
How? Purpose: Understand problems and perspectives, weigh options, and propose solutions. Topic: Parenting styles Example: How successful is each parenting style and what effect does it have on the child?		
What if? Purpose: Use the knowledge you have or learn to pose a hypothesis and consider options. Topic: Writing styles Example: What if the author chose to tell the story in a non-chronological way?		
Should? Purpose: Make a moral or practical decision based on evidence. Topic: Memoir writing Example: Should we reflect on our past experiences or is it better to focus on the future?		
Why? Purpose: Understand and explain relationships to get to the essence of a complicated issue. Topic: Social issues in literature Example: Why do we read dystopian literature, and do we need to study it in school?		

FIGURE 12. "Question lenses" handout. Adapted from *Power Tools Recharged: 125+ Essential Forms and Presentations for Your School Library Information Program* (p. 5-3A), by J. K. Valenza, 2004, Chicago, IL: American Library Association. Adapted with permission.

TYPES OF QUESTIONS
KNOWLEDGE: Write a question about the topic whose answer can be found easily. This question usually has a "correct" answer. • Which of the three little pigs was the most logical thinker?
OPEN-ENDED: Write an insightful question about the topic that will require proof and group discussion and "construction of logic" to discover or explore the answer to the question. • Why didn't the second little pig look for more stable construction materials after the first little pig's house of straw was blown down?
APPLICATION: Write a question that asks for new knowledge to be used in a different setting. • How would the story change if the wolf had tried to blow down the house made of bricks first?
CHALLENGE QUESTION: Write a question dealing with your skepticism of the author's theme, premise, etc. • How can one brother be so much smarter than his other two brothers when all three were raised in the same house?
CURIOSITY QUESTION: Write a genuine question of inquiry that springs out of your reading. • Why are so many children's stories constructed with three repetitions of events?
WORLD CONNECTION QUESTION: Write a question connecting the topic to the real world. • How can you prevent yourself from being taken advantage of when you leave your parents' home to go out and live on your own?
UNIVERSAL THEME/CORE QUESTION: Write a question dealing with a theme(s) of the text that will encourage discussion about the universality of the text. • How can we build our own defenses against evil forces?

FIGURE 13. "Types of questions" handout. Questions and descriptions taken from "Social Studies: Yo Socrates! Amend This" (p. 18), by P. S. Eisen, 2007. *School Library Media Activities Monthly, 24*(2).

- APPLICATION: Which group do you think will be the most successful out of school?

- CHALLENGE: Why do people care so much about their social rank in school, when it doesn't matter in the real world?

- CURIOSITY: Why do people label others? Do these labels affect their life? Are there these labels for kids in schools all around the world?

- WORLD CONNECTION: Why do people from groups all act the same in every school?

- UNIVERSAL THEME: What would high school be like if there were no social groups?

By pushing students to find questions that fit each type, they set themselves up to make discoveries that aren't possible through the development of a single question. Sharing by each group furthers this because it reveals the varied questions that arise from the wisdom, curiosities, and experiences of each member of the class. From here, students can choose the questions most interesting to them and add them to their ILPs.

Strategy: Modifying Questions by Changing Verbs and Nouns

Students must also learn that their initial questions will likely change as they explore and learn. We encourage this by asking them to play around with their initial questions, changing verbs and nouns to create different and sometimes

Pitfall: When Students Can't Identify a Question

If students reach a point in the process at which they have a topic they want to pursue, but they are not sure what they want to study, you can step in with some extra help. Cathy provides students with the following inquiry prompts to get them thinking about their general topic of study:

- What do you find interesting about your topic?
- How are your topics connected?
- What are the causes and effects involved in your topic?
- How has your topic changed over time?
- Why is your topic significant and to whom is it significant?
- What do you want to learn about your topic?
- What other perspectives can you consider?

By giving students these prompts, they can approach their topics in different ways, applying their own interests to their inquiries. When one of Meg's students, enrolled in British Literature, had a difficult time connecting the content of the course to his interests, she conferred with him, one on one, to help him develop his focus and, ultimately, craft an EQ. A successful football player, he could name few things other than sports that routinely grabbed his attention. Meg questioned him about how he thought people viewed football players. This led to a discussion on aggression and masculinity, which became the driving theme of his unit. From there, he began to study how the definition of masculinity has changed from the time of knights to today.

more effective questions. For example, when studying *Geeks*, Elizabeth's initial question was "What does it mean to come of age?" From there, she modified various words to create the options now listed beneath her initial question in Figure 14. By asking these questions, she approached the core of her topic— growing up—from many different angles, ultimately coming up with the EQ, "When one reaches the coming of age, does he or she make their own decisions, or do they still rely on the wisdom of others?" As with the prior activities, students can reflect on the level and purpose of each question as they determine which one works best for them. And, as in this case, the process leads them to explore a question that directly relates to where they are in life.

What I Will Read
List the core materials below. *The Geeks Shall Inherit the Earth* During your exploration, you must use additional resources to aid your inquiry. These can be pieces of literary criticism, author bios, essays about the literary movements, etc. List those additional resources below.

What I Will Learn
Please list your essential and guiding questions which you plan on pursuing this unit. EQs • When one reaches the coming of age, does he or she make their own decisions, or do they still rely on the wisdom of others? GQs • What does it mean to come of age? • What is the coming of age? • Why do we need to come of age? • How do we come of age? • What is the change that comes with the coming of age? • What is the change that comes with independence? • What is the change that comes with emotional strength? • What is the change that comes with maturity? • At what age is the coming of age?

FIGURE 14. "What I will read" and "What I will learn—Questions" from Elizabeth's ILP.

Strategy: Narrowing and Broadening Questions . . . Musically

Another way to teach question modification is through the following all-class activity used to broaden and narrow questions (see Figure 15). "Musical questions" was developed by Cathy and Marci Zane, a former librarian at Hunterdon Central. First, students write their initial question at the top of a sheet of paper. Beneath that is a table with one column for broader questions and one column for narrower questions. Music is then played, and, just like in musical chairs, students walk about the room until the music stops. They then sit in the closest seat and write down both a broader and a narrower question on their peers' papers. After a few rounds, students look at their original questions and refine or change them based on what their peers have suggested. Even if their original questions do not change, they are still left with lists of additional questions that they could use to further their inquiries.

Musical Questions: Broadening and Narrowing Our EQs

Objective: Conduct short as well as more sustained research projects to answer a question (including a self-generated question) or solve a problem; narrow or broaden the inquiry when appropriate; synthesize multiple sources on the subject, demonstrating understanding of the subject under investigation. (CCSS.ELA-LITERACY.W.9-10.7; Common Core Standards Initiative, 2010a)

My Essential Question:

_____

Peers: If you sit down to the question above when the music stops, it is your job to suggest ways to narrow and broaden it. Following the same topic, write a narrower, more specific question. Then, write a broader, more general question. Place them in the appropriate columns below.

Narrow	Broaden

FIGURE 15. "Musical questions: Broadening and narrowing our EQs" handout. Reproduced with permission from Cathy Stutzman and Marci Zane. CCSS excerpted from Common Core State Standards Initiative (2010).

Pitfall: If Students Begin by Looking for Their Answers

This model of learning is different from traditional classroom experiences because the students and the teacher have no set final answer in sight from the outset of the inquiry. This process of discovery may seem foreign to students who are used to working toward the right answer to a question proposed by the teacher rather than a question created by them. We saw many of our students choose research topics based on what they already believed and then continue to choose sources that simply reinforced that belief. To confirm this, Heather would ask the following question of most classes that visited the library for research: "How many of you, when confronted with a piece of information that disputes your original ideas about a topic, tend to ignore it?" Most students raised their hands. This is not surprising because, as Kuhlthau (2004) explained in *Seeking Meaning,* students don't always come to research with the expectation that a topic will "change" or "evolve" (p. 76). We wanted to find a way to not only give students the experience of asking genuine questions but also to give them a lot of practice in doing so. Going through this process infrequently does not give students the opportunity to begin to trust in themselves and the inquiry process, for, as Kuhlthau (2004) noted, "When the information search process is viewed as a process of construction, uncertainty and anxiety are anticipated and expected" (p. 7). Without this frame of mind, students are reluctant to pursue real questions for which there may not be an answer. That means that students' mindsets when approaching a text might need to shift from "Does this text confirm my own answer?" to "What does this text tell me about my topic, and how does it help me respond to my question?" Their responses to that second question could even lead them to completely new concepts and questions. Referring back to the ISP (Kuhlthau, 2004) is also helpful for reminding students that learning is frustrating, and by seeking only answers that confirm what they think they know, they are not really learning. Complex questions are necessary for the ILP process because they require students to move from seeking "answers" to seeking meaning.

II

Letting Go of the "One-Size-Fits-All" Lesson Plan

Enabling Students to Learn How to Learn

"Reach every student!" "Plan for different types of learners!" "Gotta get 'em all!" These are the mantras of teachers everywhere. We see them in inspirational movies: teachers who help every kid with their magnetic personalities and grit. However, reality is not like the movies. The pressure on teachers is greater than ever to devise the perfect lesson plan that reaches every student and is often what keeps us up at night. This pressure has only increased with the heightened focus on standards.*

When most people hear the word *standards*, they think of positive benchmarks that signify quality. Being told that you have standards is a good thing . . . especially when they are high standards. But the word means something very different to teachers, and those connotations are not always desirable. However, this chapter is not about the standards debate. It is about how to release yourself from the stress of having the perfect "one-size-fits-all" lesson plan and to begin using standards with students more effectively by honoring student choice and making students a more integral part of planning. This process goes beyond putting standards on the board and pushes them into the limelight so students can see "behind the curtain" and you can begin letting go of the pressure to create "one lesson plan to rule them all!"

When implementing the ILP, the second part of the "What I will learn" section deals with the skills of a unit (see Figure 16). Although students will practice every course standard, you may choose to turn over control of when and how they practice them. In this section of the book, we not only explore the benefits of this process, but we also share strategies for empowering students to work with standards and provide examples that demonstrate how the responsibility of individualizing lessons shifts from the teacher to the students.

---

*For many public schools, the objectives that shape a class are in the form of the Common Core State Standards (CCSS). Some might have additional or equivalent state objectives, course-specific proficiencies, or teacher-designed goals. For others, including private, independent, or charter schools, students might be held to objectives from organizations like the International Baccalaureate. No matter what term educators use to label them, those objectives are devised to push students to improve. For our purposes, we will refer to all of these as "standards."

What I Will Learn
Please list your essential and guiding questions that you plan on pursuing this unit.
Please list all standards that you intend on practicing this unit. Remember, choose standards that you have not already mastered since you will have to demonstrate that you are getting better as the unit progresses.

FIGURE 16. "What I will learn—Questions and standards" from the ILP. Reproduced from "The Inquiry Learning Plan: Creating Engaging Questions," by M. Donhauser, H. Hersey, C. Stutzman, and M. Zane, 2015a, *School Library Monthly* (an imprint of ABC-CLIO), *31*(3), p. 8. CC BY-NC-SA.

Students Need to Work Closely with Standards

If the purpose of standards is not made clear to students, teachers run the risk of ignoring students' needs and interests as learners. Smith, Appleman, and Wilhelm (2014) wrote about the danger of dealing with standards in isolation in their book *The Uncommon Core*:

> Creating clear and compelling purposes for learning and contexts that require and reward particular kinds of learning helps prepare students for success versus reacting to deficits. . . . Everything from vocabulary growth to deep procedural and conceptual understandings like those required by the CCSS are best achieved when students understand the purpose and immediate possibilities for using what is learned in contexts of actual use, like those provided through the use of inquiry. (p. 59)

As the authors suggest, teachers must contextualize learning so skills are not being taught in a vacuum. Personalizing the reasons and understandings through student choice and differentiation takes this one step further. When students differentiate their own learning by choosing standards, they walk away with a deep understanding of the skills they practice and how those skills make them better communicators. However, this involves a lot of practice and a lot of guidance from the teacher because students will need to grapple with the language of standards, use standards to explore a topic that is important to them, learn to self-assess and create appropriate goals, and transfer the skills to new situations.

Moving beyond Just Knowing: Standards to Challenge Every Student

Central to our thinking is the idea that "knowing what you're supposed to do doesn't mean you are able to do it" (Smith, Wilhelm, & Fredricksen, 2012, p. 20), which is why we focus on the difference between two types of knowledge:

> *Declarative knowledge* is knowledge of *what*, the kind of knowledge that can be spoken. Knowing that effective arguments need to be supported with data, or that commas follow introductory adverbial clauses is declarative knowledge. *Procedural knowledge*, on the other hand, is knowledge of *how*, a kind of knowledge that has to be performed. Being able to select the best pieces of evidence from a text requires procedural knowledge, as does the ability to compose complex sentences. (Smith et al., 2012, p. 20)

Once students know the *what* of the standards, we move beyond this declarative knowledge and work on procedural knowledge by asking students to create their own activities that help them learn *how* to meet a standard. When students design and then complete their own activities, they are encouraged to work on the content and skills that they need rather than the one-size-fits-all approach of a standard lesson plan. As Smith et al. (2014) explained:

> If students don't need scaffolding and support, then they aren't learning anything new; they are doing what they already know how to do.... Learning the new requires accessing or building resources, then applying them in new ways to the new challenge. (p. 64)

Individualized activity creation ensures that students are working on something new and then applying these new skills to a challenge geared toward their interests.

Using Standards and Activities to Increase Appropriate Risk-Taking

The one-size-fits-all approach to lesson planning does not help most students to increase their capacity for taking risks. When we ask our students how they feel about the experience of taking more control over their learning, we often see responses that indicate a discomfort with risk-taking. For example, in an anonymous course reflection, one student stated:

> I would change [the course] to a more traditional class. Where you read a book
> and have essays and discussions on it. I am not a fan of trying to teach ourselves
> and creating the rubric. I want to know what direction I am going before I start.

This is not an uncommon sentiment as we begin using inquiry with our classes, particularly from students who are "good at school."

This longing for what is already comfortable is well documented elsewhere. In his book *Excellent Sheep*, Deresiewicz (2014) explained that even students with elite educations are being "trained" to avoid risk: "The prospect of *not* being successful terrifies them, disorients them, defeats them. They have been haunted their whole lives by a fear of failure" (p. 22). Though everyone can understand this desire for comfort, learning requires a move away from what is familiar, not just in school but in life. When Warrell (2013) interviewed a variety of leaders, "The common thread of wisdom they all shared was that in today's competitive and fast-changing workplace, we can never hope to achieve success unless we're willing to embrace change and risk the discomfort of failure" (para. 3). School should be a perfect place for students to learn this lesson, being rewarded for taking risks in their work rather than being punished during assessments. However, as Lehmann has reminded us, "That doesn't mean we just hand them the blank sheet, because the blank sheet can be terrifying. It means . . . teaching them that motion from guided inquiry to open inquiry" (qtd. in TEDx Talks, 2010). When we ask students to begin choosing their own standards and ultimately creating their own activities, the responsibility of taking on their own learning path can be uncomfortable. The strategies in this section help alleviate frustration as risks are taken and mistakes are made. Using the ILP process helps students to build grit through better understanding of the standards and repeated formative attempts at activities. Together, they kick things up a notch, providing another level of individualization. Students go from choosing texts and creating questions to working with standards, creating their own rubrics, and designing activities. Instead of teachers doing all of the lesson planning, students become architects of their own learning.

Strategies for Using Standards

This chapter walks through the complex world of standards. It begins with how to select standards for study, and then moves on to using groups to help students understand and practice the standards. Last, the chapter explains how we use rubrics to increase students' knowledge of the standards and help with assessment, both by the teacher and by the student.

Strategies for Selecting Standards

Before students begin to work with the standards and add them to their ILPs, we create an abbreviated list of potential standards for a unit. In early units, this might mean a short list of four to six standards that each student practices; for later units, students might choose from a list of ten to fifteen standards based on their own individual needs. When narrowing a list of standards, we consider three questions:

1. Does the course curriculum require standards for specific texts or units?

2. Are there specific skills students will need before moving on to the next unit or class?

3. What skills will students need to practice in order to move successfully through the unit of inquiry?

These questions help us decide how much choice we can allow. Once a list is established, we ask students to select a range of standards that provides a broad spectrum for the study of both content and skills and covers the following areas: *reading, writing,* and *speaking/listening*. Choosing standards is often a collaborative process between the student and the teacher. We typically ask students to examine the list and make initial selections, and then we work with them to make sure that the selected standards are appropriately challenging. Figure 17 illustrates the instructions Meg provides her sophomore students when they select standards for their unit about *Macbeth*. Even though this is a teacher-

Standards (selected from the Common Core State Standards)

Choose one of the following standards for reading literature:

CCSS.ELA-LITERACY.RL.9-10.2: Determine a theme or central idea of a text and analyze in detail its development over the course of the text, including how it emerges and is shaped and refined by specific details; provide an objective summary of the text.

CCSS.ELA-LITERACY.RL.9-10.3: Analyze how complex characters (e.g., those with multiple or conflicting motivations) develop over the course of a text, interact with other characters, and advance the plot or develop the theme.

CCSS.ELA-LITERACY.RL.9-10.4: Determine the meaning of words and phrases as they are used in the text, including figurative and connotative meanings; analyze the cumulative impact of specific word choices on meaning and tone (e.g., how the language evokes a sense of time and place; how it sets a formal or informal tone).

Choose one of the following standards for reading informational texts:

CCSS.ELA-LITERACY.RI.9-10.6: Determine an author's point of view or purpose in a text and analyze how an author uses rhetoric to advance that point of view or purpose.

CCSS.ELA-LITERACY.RI.9-10.7: Analyze various accounts of a subject told in different mediums (e.g., a person's life story in both print and multimedia), determining which details are emphasized in each account.

Choose one of the following elements from this writing standard:

CCSS.ELA-LITERACY.W.9-10.2: Write informative/explanatory texts to examine and convey complex ideas, concepts, and information clearly and accurately through the effective selection, organization, and analysis of content.

> a) Introduce a topic; organize complex ideas, concepts, and information to make important connections and distinctions; include formatting (e.g., headings), graphics (e.g., figures, tables), and multimedia when useful to aiding comprehension.
>
> b) Develop the topic with well-chosen, relevant, and sufficient facts, extended definitions, concrete details, quotations, or other information and examples appropriate to the audience's knowledge of the topic.
>
> c) Use appropriate and varied transitions to link the major sections of the text, create cohesion, and clarify the relationships among complex ideas and concepts.
>
> d) Use precise language and domain-specific vocabulary to manage the complexity of the topic.
>
> e) Establish and maintain a formal style and objective tone while attending to the norms and conventions of the discipline in which they are writing.
>
> f) Provide a concluding statement or section that follows from and supports the information or explanation presented (e.g., articulating implications or the significance of the topic)

Choose one of the following elements for this speaking and listening standard:

CCSS.ELA-LITERACY.SL.9-10.1: Initiate and participate effectively in a range of collaborative discussions (one-on-one, in groups, and teacher-led) with diverse partners on grades 9–10 topics, texts, and issues, building on others' ideas and expressing their own clearly and persuasively.

> a) Come to discussions prepared, having read and researched material under study; explicitly draw on that preparation by referring to evidence from texts and other research on the topic or issue to stimulate a thoughtful, well-reasoned exchange of ideas.
>
> b) Work with peers to set rules for collegial discussions and decision-making (e.g., informal consensus, taking votes on key issues, presentation of alternate views), clear goals and deadlines, and individual roles as needed.
>
> c) Propel conversations by posing and responding to questions that relate the current discussion to broader themes or larger ideas; actively incorporate others into the discussion; and clarify, verify, or challenge ideas and conclusions.
>
> d) Respond thoughtfully to diverse perspectives, summarize points of agreement and disagreement, and, when warranted, qualify or justify their own views and understanding and make new connections in light of the evidence and reasoning presented.

Students are responsible for both of the following standards:

CCSS.ELA-LITERACY.W.9-10.5: Develop and strengthen writing as needed by planning, revising, editing, rewriting, or trying a new approach, focusing on addressing what is most significant for a specific purpose and audience.

CCSS.ELA-LITERACY.W.9-10.7: Conduct short as well as more sustained research projects to answer a question (including a self-generated question) or solve a problem; narrow or broaden the inquiry when appropriate; synthesize multiple sources on the subject, demonstrating understanding of the subject under investigation.

FIGURE 17. Directions for selecting standards. CCSS excerpted from Common Core State Standards Initiative (2010).

selected menu of options, it still provides differentiation by allowing students to choose which standards to practice while serving as a stepping-stone to more open choice later in the process. From this point forward, students are going to engage in a unique learning experience, and this menu of choices begins a domino effect that enables students to move toward a better understanding of their own needs as learners.

Strategy: Creating a List of Standards That Go beyond Content

When establishing a list of standards from which students can choose focus areas, some teachers may be inclined to stick to content area standards. However, there also are standards that address learning in diverse situations and across disciplines, such as:

- the American Association of School Librarians's *Standards for the 21st Century Learner* (AASL, 2007)
- an individual state's technology or learning standards
- *National Educational Technology Standards for Teachers* (International Society for Technology in Education, 2008)
- the National Council of Teachers of English's "NCTE Definition of 21st Century Literacies" (NCTE, 2013)

When coupled with content area standards, these objectives offer a range of content and skills that can broaden and deepen the curriculum. They provide opportunities to study the process of learning and practice specific skills that help students work through new information.

When choosing focus standards, we often ask our students to choose at least one standard from an abbreviated list of the AASL, the International Society for Technology in Education, and NCTE. These standards focus more on mindsets or habits and encourage students to reflect on their content acquisition as well as on the process of learning. Figure 18 offers suggested standards that cover skills associated with inquiry learning. Using standards that transcend disciplines also allows students to see connections among subjects. This helps them to transfer skills and strategies such as realizing that the reading skills they build in English will help them interpret information in science or history, or that their ability to work through the challenges of the inquiry process in social studies will help them identify times of frustration while learning how to apply new theorems in math. This transfer of knowledge and skills can be seen in reflections like that of Hayley, a tenth-grade student:

I'm using this stuff in other classes. Now I'm thinking about writing skills in Span-
ish class, and I'm synthesizing everything. I'm doing that stuff in my spare time. I'll
be watching TV and think, "Oh, that reminds me of something in *Grendel*."

(Jokingly, Hayley added, "What's wrong with me!?") When learning becomes
more natural, pervasive, and connected, students feel encouraged to apply strategies to get past hurdles, not just in their current course but in others and in life.

Skill/Habit of Mind	Standard Framework
Collaboration	ISTE-NETS, NCTE's Definition of 21st Century Literacies, Common Core ELA standards, AASL Standards for the 21st Century Learner
Reflection	AASL Standards for the 21st Century Learner
Curiosity	AASL Standards for the 21st Century Learner
Persistence	AASL Standards for the 21st Century Learner
Problem-solving	ISTE-NETS, NCTE's Definition of 21st Century Literacies, AASL Standards for the 21st Century Learner
Creativity	ISTE-NETS, AASL Standards for the 21st Century Learner
Flexibility	AASL Standards for the 21st Century Learner
Synthesis	NCTE's Definition of 21st Century Literacies, Common Core ELA standards, AASL Standards for the 21st Century Learner
Self-direction	AASL Standards for the 21st Century Learner
Information and Digital Literacy	ISTE-NETS, NCTE's Definition of 21st Century Literacies, Common Core ELA standards, AASL Standards for the 21st Century Learner

FIGURE 18. Options for choosing standards that are not discipline or content specific. Standard frameworks
from AASL (2007), Common Core State Standards Initiative [CCSSI] (various), International Society for
Technology in Education (2008), and NCTE (2013).

Strategy: Using Diagnostics to Help Students Choose Standards

We all want students to practice and progress in skill areas that need the most
improvement rather than simply showcase what they already know again and
again. For students to do that, especially when selecting their own standards,
they must understand their strengths and weaknesses. At the beginning of a

course, we administer diagnostic assessments to get a pulse on their abilities in the core areas of reading, writing, and speaking/listening.

A unit's diagnostic assesses possible content and skills that the students could practice throughout the unit, which would be specified in the list of potential standards that you have selected. Once you have chosen standards, the diagnostic should provide enough questions in each of those content or skill areas to get an accurate demonstration of students' abilities. The example shown in Figure 19 is a reading diagnostic from a sophomore honors English class that was preparing to study *The Catcher in the Rye*. Diagnostic assignments in speaking/listening and in writing could stem from the same reading (examples of these assessments can be found in the online appendix).

This reading diagnostic assesses more than content; it goes beyond what the student knows about the text to explore their process of understanding the text. The instructions ask students to demonstrate the strategies that they use as they read and set them up to answer the analysis questions, which are aligned to the requirements of the reading standards. Their responses in this section can then reveal competency or areas for improvement. Finally, the self-reflection at the end provides additional information about reading habits and interests. This assessment identifies areas of weakness and aligns them to a specific standard that the student can practice throughout the unit. For Jenna, who struggled to answer the second analysis question, Cathy suggested she focus on the following standard:

CCSS.ELA-Literacy.RL.9-10.1: Cite strong and thorough textual evidence to support analysis of what the text says explicitly as well as inferences drawn from the text. (CCSSI, 2010)

After they completed the reading diagnostic, Cathy asked students to discuss the text in small groups and write an essay connecting the text to another source. Using these as speaking and writing diagnostics, she assessed the specific skills that students would practice throughout the upcoming unit, and, with each one, students made connections between an area of weakness and a skill outlined by a standard. Through this practice, students begin to set goals for improvement and become more familiar with the specific requirements needed to meet those goals. If using the ILP, students can write those goals or standards into the "What I will learn" section, just as Jenna did in the excerpt from her ILP (Figure 20). The standards, coupled with the EQs and GQs, serve as a constant foundation for the student's unit activities and reflections.

Honors Sophomore Diagnostic Reading

Actively read the *New York* magazine article "Why You Never Truly Leave High School" by Jennifer Senior and show the process of your reading. You may annotate, ask questions, evaluate claims, connect points to your own or others' experiences, or use any other strategies that help you to make meaning of the reading. Then, respond to the analysis questions below.

Analysis Questions:
1. What is the main idea of the text? How do you know? What reasons or details does the author use to support her argument?
2. Identify a section of the text in which the author implies a stance, but does not come right out and say it. Why do you think she chooses not to be more forthcoming?
3. How does the text's structure enhance or develop the argument? How does the argument shift or change as the paragraphs go on?
4. Circle important words or phrases that contribute to the argument of the text. What tone do they present, and how do they impact the overall meaning?
5. Describe the author and her purpose for writing the article. How does this information shape the style of the text?
6. Are there any points in which the author's perspective interferes with her ability to provide sound reasoning for her arguments?
7. What is the weakest part of her argument, and why?

Reading Reflection: Once you have completed the reading activity, you will need to reflect on your reading abilities. This will help us develop reading goals for your time in the course, and it will also help me to determine which skills we will focus on during our first unit. Please respond ***honestly*** to the questions below.

1. When you read "Why You Never Truly Leave High School," what strategies did you use, if any? For example, did you re-read any portions? Did you visualize what you were reading? Did you hear the voice of the speaker in your head as you read? Did you annotate the text? Did you use some other strategy?
2. When you read outside of school, do you tend to read nonfiction texts like essays, newspaper/magazine articles, memoirs, and biographies, or do you tend to read fictional texts like novels, poetry, and plays?
3. What was the last complete book you read for fun? When did you read it?
4. What kinds of texts do you struggle with the most?

This activity and reflection will be formatively assessed and used to develop reading goals for the first unit. While this will not receive a grade, you want to be sure to really show off your best reading abilities.

FIGURE 19. Sample reading diagnostic.

What I Will Learn
Please list your essential and guiding questions which you plan on pursuing this unit. EQs How does bullying affect a person? GQs What is the correlation between the type of bullying and the effect on a person? What causes people to interpret bullying differently? What are the short term and long term effects of bullying? How do the effects of bullying on a perpetrator compare to the effects of bullying on a victim?
Please list all standards that you intend on practicing this unit. Remember, choose standards that you have not already mastered since you will have to demonstrate that you are getting better as the unit progresses. CCSS.ELA-LITERACY.RL.9-10.1: Cite strong and thorough textual evidence to support analysis of what the text says explicitly as well as inferences drawn from the text. CCSS.ELA-LITERACY.W.9-10.1.E: Provide a concluding statement or section that follows from and supports the argument presented. CCSS.ELA-LITERACY.SL.9-10.3: Evaluate a speaker's point of view, reasoning, and use of evidence and rhetoric, identifying any fallacious reasoning or exaggerated or distorted evidence. CCSS.ELA-LITERACY.SL.9-10.6: Adapt speech to a variety of contexts and tasks, demonstrating command of formal English when indicated or appropriate. CCSS.ELA-LITERACY.L.9-10.3: Apply knowledge of language to understand how language functions in different contexts, to make effective choices for meaning or style, and to comprehend more fully when reading or listening. CCSS.ELA-LITERACY.L.9-10.3.A: Write and edit work so that it conforms to the guidelines in a style manual (e.g., *MLA Handbook*, Turabian's *Manual for Writers*) appropriate for the discipline and writing type.

FIGURE 20. "What I will learn" from Jenna's ILP (to see Jenna's full ILP for this unit, please refer to the online appendix). CCSS excerpted from CCSSI (2010).

Strategies for Tackling the Standards Together

After selecting standards, students still need a better understanding of what they mean before beginning to work with them. Because standards might be unfamiliar to many students, we set up opportunities for students to work together as they familiarize themselves with standard language and establish criteria for meeting their requirements. This is important to do whether or not you are implementing the ILP. Barron and Darling-Hammond (2008) cited numerous studies that acknowledge the benefits of student collaboration and explained that "most recently, the focus has gone beyond the practical benefits of collaboration for individual learning to recognize the importance of helping children develop the capacity to collaborate as necessary for preparation for all kinds of work" (p. 19). Furthermore, Harvey and Daniels (2009) detailed how to use collaboration in the pursuit of questions; they suggested thinking of "literature circles—but instead of choosing a single book to read, kids select a topic or a question to explore" (p. 13). They proposed the idea of using "inquiry circles." We use the same name but expand the use of these groupings beyond topics and questions to exploring skills and standards. Initially, full classes may be working on the same standards, so inquiry circles can help students work through the language of the standards. However, you can also break students into circles determined by individual standard needs. Figure 21 demonstrates the standard choices made by students in Cathy's tenth-grade English class after taking diagnostic tests. Their choices dictated how the students were grouped. As the students studied different skills throughout the unit, they shifted groups—reading one day, writing the next, speaking after that.

In this example, one student, Naveen, chose to work on the standards CCSS. ELA-Literacy.RL.9-10.3 ("RL 3" in Figure 21), CCSS.ELA-Literacy.W.9-10.1.a ("W 1a"), and CCSS.ELA-Literacy.SL.9-10.3 ("SL 3") (CCSSI, 2010). On the first day, Cathy asked for students to meet with reading groups, so Naveen worked with Charlotte. He later met with Lucas and Ryan to work on writing skills, and then, on another day, with Vikram, Charlotte, Alexa, Harper, and Josie to practice speaking and listening. Over the course of the unit, Naveen worked with seven different students specifically grouped to help one another through new and potentially uncomfortable skills.

Collaboration is especially helpful here because students may be working on skills that they have never attempted before or in which they feel inadequate. Giving them a group within which everyone is experiencing similar feelings can

RL 1	RL 2	RL 3	RL 4	RL 5	RL 7	RL 9	W1a	W1b	W1c	W1d	W1e	W1f	SL 1	SL 2	SL 3	SL 4
Jacob	Benjamin	Charlotte	Hannah	Chloe	Lucas	Jaidyne	Lucas	Claire	Vikram	Lorenzo	Chloe	Alexander	Lucas	Claire	Vikram	Myara
Olivia	Faris	Naveen	Lorenzo	Dylan	Avery	Harper	Naveen	Jacob	Alexa	Harper	Olivia	Dylan	Olivia	Jacob	Charlotte	Chloe
Ryan	Alexa		Vikram	Mason	Noah	Myara	Ryan	Charlotte	Avery	Jaidyne	Benjamin		Jaidyne	Hannah	Alexa	Avery
Claire			Alexander	Emily		Josie			Hannah	Emily			Faris	Dylan	Harper	Lorenzo
									Josie	Noah			Alexander		Naveen	Ryan
													Noah		Josie	Emily

FIGURE 21. Inquiry circle groupings by standard choices.

alleviate the apprehension they might feel if they were working with students who are proficient in those areas. Students in Naveen's groups used many of the strategies discussed below to explore the intricacies of the skill requirements and to ultimately design activities that would help them progress.

Strategy: Close-Reading of the Standards

Once standards are selected, the next step in working with them is to delve further into their language. Standards are written for teachers. What's more, many students have never seen actual standards. Some educational theorists (e.g., Moss, Brookhart, & Long, 2011; Wiggins, 2013) have suggested breaking down standards for our students and displaying them on agendas or on the board in "student-friendly" language. However, Wiggins (2013) cautioned that posting them "isn't the point." Instead:

> The aim is to ensure that students understand goals and how current activities support those goals. Ideally, then, the student has perspective and sees value in the work: they understand the *why* of the current work in order to find it more meaningful and to facilitate purposeful learning, and they have a touchstone for gauging progress (and thus use of time). ("Effective vs. ineffective goal-setting," para. 1)

The following strategies encourage students to do the work that Wiggins suggests, making students' understanding deeper and their use of standards more impactful.

Providing time to examine the academic language helps students understand what will be expected of them. We divide students into inquiry circles to complete "close-reads" of the standard and its language, breaking it down in two ways:

1. Thinking about actions
    - What is the standard requiring you to *do*?
    - What *actions* will you take to meet it?

2. Discussing products or evidence of the standard
    - What is the standard asking you to *produce*?
    - What will this work look like?
    - What should you be able to *show* that proves you've completed the actions above?

Figure 22 demonstrates a model close-reading of the AASL Standard 1.1.3 ("Develop and refine a range of questions to frame the search for new understanding"; AASL, 2007, p. 4). We provide this for students to see how they might explore *actions* and *products*. For this standard, verbs like *develop, refine,* and *frame* might be familiar, but, when pressed to explain what those actions look like, students may have a hard time conceptualizing them. Basically, they have the declarative knowledge but not the procedural knowledge. To remedy that, we ask students to research the words and list synonyms, definitions, or questions. In this example, the verb *refine* is defined as follows: "To make stronger . . . to make it classier or cleaner." It is also interpreted as to make "clearer."

Once the verb's meaning is established, students can then go on to brainstorm what kinds of actions they can take to demonstrate those verbs. In our sample standard, students needed to demonstrate that they were changing the question because of new experiences. To do that, students might first list ques-

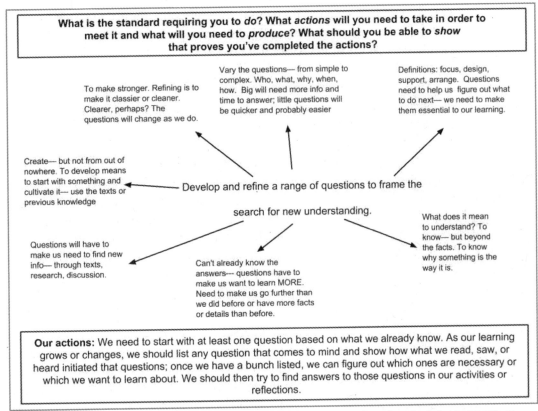

FIGURE 22. Model of a close-reading for AASL Standard 1.1.3. Excerpted from *Standards for the 21st Century Learner* by the American Association of School Librarians, a division of the American Library Association, copyright © 2007 American Library Association. Used with permission. Adapted from "The Inquiry Learning Plan: The Role of Standards," by M. Donhauser, H. Hersey, C. Stutzman, and M. Zane, 2015b, *School Library Monthly* (an imprint of ABC-CLIO), *31*(4), p. 10. CC BY-NC-SA.

tions that come to mind as they read, then write down new information (quotes, examples, experiences) that changes the way they are thinking, and, last, show edits and revisions to the questions that are linked to the new information. They might also write brief explanations as to why they eliminated questions from their original lists.

Because a standard close-read involves looking up words and brainstorming actions and products, this may take fifteen to twenty minutes. However, after practice, students can move more quickly through this process in subsequent units. The teacher should check for understanding and provide feedback on these close-reads through whole-class discussion (if the standard is common), small-group review, or in writing before the next class meeting.

Strategy: Drawing the Standards

Another way to supplement the close-reading of a standard is for students to draw its required actions. This helps them to visualize the actions it requires and really identify what it is they will be asked to perform. For example, consider standard CCSS.ELA-Literacy.RL.9-10.3:

> Analyze how complex characters (e.g., those with multiple or conflicting motivations) develop over the course of a text, interact with other characters, and advance the plot or develop the theme. (CCSSI, 2010)

FIGURE 23. Drawing the standards sample from students.

When asked to simply identify verbs, students might initially underline words such as *develop* or *advance*. And, while those are certainly actions they should understand in the larger context of the skill, those are not actions *they* will need to perform in order to meet the standard requirements. Their action is "analyze." Working in small groups, they can then draw the verb *analyze*. They may need to look up the word and determine its nuances rather than rely on previous experience or a cursory understanding. One group shared the image in Figure 23 with the class. In their rationale, the group members explained that, to them, analyzing meant the obvious examining of information, but that it went beyond simply looking at it. They had to use different lenses to interpret the information, examining the information from new angles and perspectives to get a more comprehensive understanding.

After visualizing the actions of the standard, students can more easily see themselves performing the tasks and can identify the other verbs in the standard to figure out who or what is performing those actions. In the case of standard CCSS.ELA-Literacy.RL.9-10.3 (CCSSI, 2010), the additional verbs are *develop*, *interact*, and *advance*, but students need to determine that those are being performed by the character, not by them as readers. Once they make that distinction, students see that the actions of the characters are the things they need to analyze when performing the skill of the standard.

Strategies for Developing Student Rubrics

After becoming familiar with a standard through a close-reading exercise, students have a more than cursory understanding of its requirements, but they further increase their familiarity with the intricacies of a standard's language by creating their own rubrics. Designing rubrics is also another step toward students gaining an accurate understanding of their own abilities because it gives them insight into evaluation criteria. Though students gain clarity on the nuances of many words like *analyze* or *evaluate* after doing a close-reading, in order to make an accurate rubric, students need to do more than paste these sometimes hackneyed words into columns with accompanying adjectives. They need to align the standard's requirements with measurable criteria for valid assessment. Again, drawing attention to the actions and the products is essential.

Because the language of the standards can be difficult, students will likely benefit from working through them together in inquiry circles. Working only with students who are focused on the same criteria provides a common sense of purpose, and students can work together to create a common language for and ownership of the requirements. We start by giving them a blank template with three categories: "Advanced proficient," "Proficient," and "Developing" (see Figure 24). We equate those to A range, C range, and F range, respectively; anything that straddles proficiency levels earns grades of B or D. "Proficient" work, we tell them, is meeting the standard. Work in this range shows competency with the requirements of the standard. "Advanced proficient" should extend the standard, not just do more of it. We discuss and use the strategies discussed in the following sections to explain what it means to go beyond the requirements, not simply to meet them. Last, work in the "Developing" category falls short of demonstrating proficiency. We make sure to explain to students that the "Developing" category is common when learning a new skill.

Use your standard to describe the qualities of work that is "Advanced Proficient," "Proficient," and "Developing." You may use the language of the standard for the "Proficient" column. Then you will need to figure out ways in which someone could go beyond expectations for the "Advanced Proficient" column and ways in which a student might fall short of proficiency for the "Developing" column. Write your descriptions in the columns below.

Standard:

Advanced Proficient	Proficient	Developing

FIGURE 24. Template for creating a standards rubric.

As every teacher knows, rubric creation is an extremely difficult skill. When students attempt it with a standards rubric, they usually take one or both of these missteps:

1. Diminish and deplete the standard requirements when describing "Proficient." When they think "C," they think work in that range should not meet requirements.

2. Differentiate "Advanced proficient" from "Proficient" with words like *successfully* or *thoroughly* without explanation.

Neither of those is an accurate or assessable option, however. As we point out, a C is an average grade; it is passing, and, therefore, work in the "Proficient" range should meet the requirements of the standard itself. Additionally, simply adding adverbs to the "Advanced proficient" column does not explain *how* it is improved. Figure 25 demonstrates a group's first attempts at a rubric for standard CCSS.ELA-Literacy.RL.9-10.1:

Cite strong and thorough textual evidence to support analysis of what the text says explicitly as well as inferences drawn from the text. (CCSSI, 2010)

Advanced Proficient	Proficient
• Makes a strong claim and thoroughly supports it through accurate quotes from the text • Accurately infers ideas throughout the entire novel using bountiful amounts of evidence • Cites all textual evidence used in the piece with proper citation	• Makes a claim and supports it through actual quotes coming from the text • Infers ideas about the story using evidence from the text • Textual evidence supports and furthers the piece • Cites all textual evidence used

FIGURE 25. Students' first attempt at rubric creation.

This initial rubric misses the mark in two ways. In an attempt to differentiate between "Proficient" and "Advanced proficient," the students watered down the "Proficient" level by removing the idea of thoroughness. Furthermore, when using adverbs like *thoroughly* or other qualifying adjectives in "Advanced proficient," they needed to be able to explain what it looks like. The strategies that follow describe ways to help students articulate the skill requirements more clearly to improve their rubrics and their understanding.

Strategy: Using the Common Core to Develop Rubric Criteria

To help students differentiate between levels of the rubric, we use the CCSS as examples of gradated skills. The CCSS provide models of how language can be used to change the criteria for each grade level. They are designed in a band so that each specific standard always has the same core element across grade levels; it just becomes increasingly sophisticated and complex. So, students can examine the standard's language for different grade levels and get a sense of where they should have already gained proficiency and where they will be aiming in future years.

Figure 26 shows the changes in requirements for standard CCSS.ELA-Literacy.RL.1 from eighth to ninth–tenth grades (bolded) and then from ninth–tenth to eleventh–twelfth grades (underlined). Some changes are subtle, like the shift

Grade 8	Grade 9-10	Grade 11-12
CCSS.ELA-LITERACY.RL.8.1 Cite the textual evidence that most strongly supports an analysis of what the text says explicitly as well as inferences drawn from the text.	CCSS.ELA-LITERACY.RL.9-10.1 Cite **strong and thorough** textual evidence to support analysis of what the text says explicitly as well as inferences drawn from the text.	CCSS.ELA-LITERACY.RL.11-12.1 Cite strong and thorough textual evidence to support analysis of what the text says explicitly as well as inferences drawn from the text, <u>including determining where the text leaves matters uncertain.</u>

FIGURE 26. Grade-level variations for standard CCSS.ELA-Literacy.RL.1 (with bolding and underlining added for emphasis). CCSS excerpted from CCSSI (2010).

from "Cite the textual evidence that most strongly supports an analysis" to "Cite strong and thorough textual evidence to support analysis." Closely studying that shift will allow students to think about the meaning of *strong* and *thorough* and determine why the ninth–tenth grade version is more sophisticated. There are more obvious additions to requirements, like those for the eleventh–twelfth grades. Students are now expected not only to provide support for "inferences drawn from the text," but they must also consider "where the text leaves matters uncertain." In this case, there is an obvious progression from one grade level to the next. Students in ninth grade can use the requirements for eleventh and twelfth graders to describe how they might go above and beyond the requirements for their age group. They could also point out where they might fall short of the ninth–tenth-grade standard by describing the requirements of the eighth-grade standard.

The group from Figure 25 that was examining standard CCSS.ELA-Literacy.RL.1 used the eleventh–twelfth-grade version to revise their "Advanced proficient" description and established the criteria outlined in Figure 27. Now they can easily demonstrate the difference between "Advanced proficient" and their original description of "Proficient" work.

This provides a unique challenge for students in the eleventh and twelfth grades, however, because they do not have higher grade-level standards to use for ideas. Instead, we can guide them to increase difficulty by adding supplementary or more challenging sources, requiring a more purposeful application of the skill, or combining the skill with another.

Original Rubric	
Advanced Proficient	**Proficient**
• Makes a strong claim and thoroughly supports it through accurate quotes from the text • Accurately infers ideas throughout the entire novel using bountiful amounts of evidence • Cites all textual evidence used in the piece with proper citation	• Makes a claim and supports it through actual quotes coming from the text • Infers ideas about the story using evidence from the text • Textual evidence supports and furthers the piece • Cites all textual evidence used

Revised Rubric	
Advanced Proficient	**Proficient**
• Uses evidence from the text to answer questions the author might leave in a reader's mind • Draws in support from other sources • Determines whether text left matters uncertain by inferring ideas from the surrounding text	• Makes a claim and supports it through actual passages coming from the text • Infers ideas about the story using evidence from the text • Textual evidence supports and furthers the piece • Cites all textual evidence used by using quotation marks and in text citation

FIGURE 27. Rubric revisions.

Pitfall: Misconceptions about the Original Intention of the Standard

When creating rubrics, teachers and students should be careful not to stray too far from the original intention of the standard when they develop their criteria. For example, if a student is creating a rubric for standard CCSS.ELA-Literacy.SL.9-10.5:

> Make strategic use of digital media (e.g., textual, graphical, audio, visual, and interactive elements) in presentations to enhance understanding of findings, reasoning, and evidence and to add interest. (CCSSI, 2010)

they might be tempted to make additions like "Speak[ing] about the topic without reading from notes." Of course, this is an important skill, but it has little to do with incorporating media into presentations, which is at the crux of the standard. By focusing on individual standard skills, students can hone those traits in their work, take risks to improve in those areas, and not worry quite as much about other skills. Therefore, students should be encouraged to focus only on what's in the standard when creating rubrics.

Additional skills can be practiced by selecting additional standards as any individual student sees fit. In this case, if a student wanted to practice speaking without notes, she might also choose to practice standard CCSS.ELA-Literacy.SL.9-10.1.a:

> Come to discussions prepared, having read and researched material under study; explicitly draw on that preparation by referring to evidence from texts and other research on the topic or issue to stimulate a thoughtful, well-reasoned exchange of ideas. (CCSSI, 2010)

Alternately, a student who needs practice with spelling and grammar in written parts of a presentation might add another standard:

> CCSS.ELA-Literacy.L.9-10.2.c: Spell correctly. (CCSSI, 2010)

By selecting and practicing an appropriate mix of standards and objectives, students can individualize their learning in any given unit, but, as we remind students during rubric creation, the rubrics for each standard need to focus solely on the skill(s) covered by that standard.

Strategy: Using Model Work to Develop Rubric Criteria

Students also examine sample work in each skill area to accurately articulate a standard's nuances and hash out developmental levels within the rubric. Models and professional examples can help them see differences between exemplary work and the "Proficient" work described by the standards. For example, in one sophomore class, students were working with standard CCSS.ELA-Literacy. SL.9-10.5:

> Make strategic use of digital media (e.g., textual, graphical, audio, visual, and interactive elements) in presentations to enhance understanding of findings, reasoning, and evidence and to add interest. (CCSSI, 2010)

They got stuck on the phrase "to add interest." They weren't sure what it meant or what that looked like. Allowing students to see this skill in action was the best way for them to understand the difference between the language of the standard (labeled as "Proficient" on the rubric) and the language of what "Advanced proficient" looked like in that skill area.

Cathy suggested that students watch a YouTube clip of an audience reacting to a multimedia presentation and track what the crowd was doing to show interest and what the presenter was doing to cause that reaction. Rather than relying on frequency as the distinguishing criteria in a rubric, they had language to describe what the skill looks like. In other words, they began focusing on quality and not just quantity. After seeing the speaker in the clip "make strategic use of digital media," they knew what they needed to replicate, and they could describe what it looks like to carefully place media in their presentations at the points that most require the audience's attention. Specifically, they realized that:

- They had to make clear the purpose of the media to their audience.
- They needed to select media that not only supported their points but also met the audience at its level of understanding and drew on its interests.
- If their multimedia presentations were working, audience members would act similarly to the audience in the model videos.

The resulting rubric (see Figure 28), written by Preeti, Dana, and Kristen, encompasses and articulates these multiple requirements. These three students took the language of the standard and put it into terms they could understand. Even the "Proficient" column, which encompasses the standard requirements, has been rewritten by the students. In this example, "Developing" describes a student's early attempts at a presentation involving digital media where some sources might be inappropriate for an audience or the audience loses interest. "Advanced proficient" extends the original standard by involving specific audience reactions like questions, commentary, and shifts in original opinions.

Strategy: Collecting Rubrics throughout a Course

Because students spend a lot of time and effort on their close-reads and their rubrics, it seems a shame to discard them at the end of a unit simply because they aren't practicing that standard anymore. Not to mention, the teacher becomes accustomed to its layout and its requirements. Therefore, one way to preserve the work, give it even more credibility, and save the teacher and students time and effort is to reuse rubrics for the rest of the class once they are created. Take, for example, Preeti, Dana, and Kristen's rubric for the speaking and listening standard (Figure 28); the students who chose that standard for the next unit used that same rubric. However, to make sure that they felt ownership over the requirements and that they had the same level of deep understanding that Preeti's group did, the new students had an opportunity to perform a close-read and rework any aspect of the rubric. Essentially, the students' work developed into classwide rubrics that were respected as functional assessment tools but remained malleable and collaborative.

Advanced Proficient	Proficient	Developing
• Uses media purposefully to enhance/add to findings, reasoning, and evidence • Uses digital media that is appropriate for the audience and relates to their interests • Uses a variety of media for evidence to appeal to diversity of interests/ understandings within an audience • Makes the presentation interactive – incites questions, participation, shifts in thoughts/opinions, and/or thoughtful commentary • Analyzes and discusses media to connect it to reasoning and overall topic/argument • Presenter is well-prepared and can speak about the topic without reading from notes. • Speaks clearly while presenting	• Uses digital media to provide elaboration on key findings, evidence, and reasons • Makes the presentation interesting by using media that relates to audience members • Allows for questions, participation, commentary • Presenter is prepared • Speaks clearly while presenting; presentation is easy to understand	• Uses few digital media texts while presenting OR does not use media to elaborate on key ideas • Loses audience's attention. • Does not use a variety of sources OR uses sources that are inappropriate for the audience • All of the information is written on a presentation source like powerpoint and presenter simply reads from it • Difficult to follow; disorganized

FIGURE 28. Student rubric for standard CCSS.ELA-Literacy.SL.9-10.5. CCSS excerpted from CCSSI (2010).

Strategies for Creating Activities

5

So far, this book has explored how students can take responsibility for aspects of their English class experience, specifically by choosing texts, creating questions, and working with standards. Each of the components can be added to an ILP or completed separately. But, for students to be in control of the way they learn, they should bring all of these components together to create their own activities, which serve as practice before a final assessment. This is where the ILP really comes alive, as it is used to track not only texts, questions, and standards but also the activities students create and the reflections they use to chart their progress.

In traditional classroom settings, students are often given activities with the criteria laid out for them. However, when students understand what a standard is asking them to produce, they can begin to conceive these activities on their own. With the ILP approach, designing an activity is an act of synthesis: create and complete an assignment that attempts to answer a question while practicing a standard. That is no easy task, and this is the point in the process where the majority of students struggle.

We reassure our students that much of the thinking around designing activities is done when they examine the standards, and so we recommend that they review their close-reads of the standards and/or their rubrics, whether student- or teacher-created. Revisiting the criteria, as well as the verbs and nouns used in the rubric, allows students to figure out what they will need to do to practice the skills that are normally taught by the teacher. It's through multiple attempts at the skills and responses to feedback that students will ultimately demonstrate that they are meeting the requirements.

Creating individual activities can be done in stages, moving from full-class activities to activities designed in inquiry circles to independent activities, with students gaining more and more responsibility as the class progresses. As students move into more individualized work, an array of strategies provides scaffolding for them to devise their own activities (see Figure 29). As with all the strategies in this book, you may choose to use the ones in this section individually or as part of the ILP. If implementing the ILP, designing activities comes

Student Growth: The Learning Process and Reflections
Learning Activities: Throughout the course of the unit, you will complete nine activities. By the end of the ILP, you will be synthesizing what you've learned about your texts and research to help you better understand the essential questions, and all of the standards must be addressed at least once in each round.
Activity 1:
Activity 2:
Activity 3:
EQ Reflection 1: How do your texts and research help you answer your questions? What do you still need to learn?
Standards Reflection 1: What progress have you made toward your standards? What do you still need to learn?

FIGURE 29. Student growth: The learning process and reflections. Adapted from "The Role of Reflection in the Inquiry Plan," by M. Donhauser, H. Hersey, C. Stutzman, and M. Zane, 2015c, *School Library Monthly* (an imprint of ABC-CLIO), *31*(6), p. 8. CC BY-NC-SA.

after students have determined the three main building blocks: (1) selecting a text or texts, (2) developing questions, and (3) choosing standards to practice. Activities in the ILP come in rounds of three—the first two rounds are for formative practice and the last for summative grading. These rounds are coupled with opportunities for reflection, which we talk about in Chapter 7.

Strategy: Designing Activities as a Class

Creating their first activity is often difficult for students, so we highly recommend developing it together as a class. Usually, we begin by designing an activity together for a single standard, as Meg did when her class was working on standard CCSS.ELA-Literacy.RL.11-12.1 (CCSSI, 2010). They used the rubric shown in Figure 30 to develop their activity. Although this rubric does break some of our guidelines about qualifying adjectives, the students establish criteria for "Advanced proficient" that require them to develop a theory and explain what they see in the text that serves as evidence (especially where the evidence may be abstract or implied).

Using the criteria in their rubric as a guide, students brainstormed in small groups first and then proposed activities to the rest of the class. We ask students to make these activities applicable to any text since they will be choosing a variety of texts. Because students require a lot of coaching as they create activities

Standard	Advanced Proficient	Proficient	Developing
1. Cite strong and thorough textual evidence to support analysis of what the text says explicitly as well as inferences drawn from the text, including determining where the text leaves matters uncertain.	Creates an elaborate understanding of the material using sources. Reader has a sophisticated understanding of the text and uses strong textual evidence from throughout texts to support theories. Uses quotes to further understanding. Able to explain the material including ideas that may be left to interpretation.	Able to use specific text and resource information to support understanding of the material. Able to read between the lines. Explains where the material is being clear and where it allows for interpretation. Explains how the info supports the purpose. Moves beyond summary.	Basic understanding of text; vague insights; supported with very little textual evidence. Does not attempt connections deeper than the text; simple restatement of text. Misinterprets text.

FIGURE 30. Student-designed rubric for standard CCSS.ELA-Literacy.RL.11-12.1. CCSS excerpted from CCSSI (2010).

for the first time, Meg conferenced with each group to guide them through the process, referring back to the rubric and the language of the standards. But, even with the help of a learning community, some of the first attempts fell short of their rubric's expectations:

- Visualizing with media
- Get quotes from the text and draw what it means
- Hollywood Squares—people are contestants and the authors are the people who get asked questions
- Draw with friends!
- Telephone game
- Skits based off of text
- Board game
- Cooking
- Check your understanding squares

Activities such as "Draw with friends!" and "Cooking" don't provide the opportunity for the depth of text analysis required by the standard. So the class went back to this list and compared the ideas against the criteria in the rubric to think about which ones could work and why. After limiting the choices, the class voted on the remaining activities. Ultimately, they decided to do the last one, a type of graphic organizer for students to "cite . . . evidence to support analysis" and make "inferences . . . including determining where the text leaves matters uncertain."

Figure 31 is an example of how one student used the activity generated by the class. It's an excerpt from Juliet's response to "The Poisoned Apple," from Sir Thomas Malory's *Le Morte d'Arthur*. Meg's comments in the margin ask questions that help Juliet develop her thinking to show greater competency in the reading standard during future attempts at the skill. Juliet chose to take this feedback and make improvements in this skill when she attempted the standard for her next text. At that point, she used the same graphic organizer with a new text, but she could have tried something totally different, as long as it still worked to meet the standard. To see Juliet's progress with this standard as well as how she examined multiple texts with this particular activity format, please visit her complete ILP in the online appendix.

Even when activities are determined as a class, students are always responsible for their own work. Completing these individually means that students demonstrate their own abilities with the skill and can focus on content that is important to them. In this case, even if students are reading different texts or exploring different questions, they can still complete the student-designed graphic organizer.

What happened? (Quote and Summary)	What does it mean? (What does it mean in the broader context of the text?)	Establish a deeper connection (Connect to previous knowledge, experience, ect.)	Create a conclusion (What does it mean in a broader context)		
"But ever his thoughts privily were on the queen, and so they loved together more hotter than they did to forehand, and had many such privy draughts together that many in the court spake of it." - The Queen and Sir Lancelot had a forbidden romance that some people in the court knew about	I think on some level the queen was unhappy and she had turned to Lancelot for love. The court gossiped about it, but I think that also the king was just oblivious to everything and maybe she was rebelling against that as well	i don't have any experience with marriage, but I find that with parents sometimes kids do things just to rebel against them. Maybe the queen and king were unhappy, or maybe she just wanted to go and cheat on him because he wouldn't know.	I think the king having no idea what's really happening happens a lot throughout the text. This might be a motive for some of the things that happen, or maybe it's just for comic relief or to let the reader feel like they're in on a secret	**Meg Donhauser** 7:04 PM Feb 6, 2013 Resolve What makes you think that? Something in the text, prior knowledge? **Meg Donhauser** 7:14 PM Feb 6, 2013 Resolve This is an interesting idea--does it endear you to either character?	

FIGURE 31. Student-designed activity called "Check your understanding squares."

When Do They Read?

There are many entry points to the ILP, which means that the order in which students address question development, standards work, text selection, activity creation, and reading their texts can vary. No matter what approach you decide to take, reading the texts and completing activities almost always occur in tandem.

Let's take Shea, from Chapter 3, for example. In the short story unit, students in his class first examined the standards, which helped to create GQs about writing. Once Shea developed his EQ based on the GQs, he chose individual short stories to read. But before he started reading, he designed his activities. Because the unit's questions and skills were applicable to any short story and were based on skills and not the specific texts, he was able to create them prior to reading. He was then able to read the short stories throughout the unit and complete the reading activities using those texts.

Some students start with their texts, especially if it is a common text. The text itself will inspire questions, so students may read a chapter or two before they develop EQs and GQs. Elizabeth, whose questions are showcased in Chapter 3, used the first chapter of *The Geeks Shall Inherit the Earth* to develop both types of questions. She did her initial reading outside of school, and then completed standard close-reads and rubric development in class. Once she understood the skills and questions for the unit, she developed her activities for Round 1. Because *Geeks* is a long text, she divided it into three equal portions, covering a third of each text during each round of activities.

If students begin with personal experience and interests, they might develop questions first that guide them through text selection. For example, Mike, from Chapter 1, began his study of American Romantic literature by creating questions about the power of nature and its relationship to humans. He then selected short and long texts over the course of two class periods in the school's library. While he and his classmates delved into their books at home, they read their short pieces in class during sustained silent reading time, and they used those texts and their standards to begin developing activities. Mike drew from his book in almost every speaking activity and in his later rounds of reading activities, making connections between the themes and craft of the book and those of the shorter poems and short stories.

Strategy: Prompting Students to Synthesize Content and Skills

To help students as they create activities throughout the course, Meg developed guiding prompts (see Figure 32) to remind them that their activity must include their text, questions, and standards. Even if some of these are teacher selected, students can still design their own activities. Meg uses this explanation either early in the process or when students are really struggling because it is very guided.

As you create and complete your activity, you need to keep three elements in mind: the text, an essential question, and the standards.

- In most cases, your text is an independent read of a long text. You might also be reading articles, essays, poems, short stories, etc. On occasion, your text might be a film or tv show, a piece of music or artwork, or even a class discussion.

- Your EQ is one that relates to your text on a philosophical or personal level. For example, a question might be, "How can guilt affect future decisions?" So, for this activity you would want to pull passages that will eventually help you answer your essential question — passages about guilt or decision-making. This helps you focus on what's important in a text!

- Your standards deal with specific aspects of reading, writing, speaking/listening, and inquiry. Your first step is to understand what the standards are asking you to do and what to produce. For example, Reading Standard 5 deals with author's choices, structure, plot sequence, and overall meaning. The standard is telling you to analyze the order of events and to produce evidence of this analysis using examples from throughout the text. So you will need to have specific quotes with some type of analysis. Questions you might ask yourself include: How did the author sequence the events and how does the sequence relate to the overall message of the book? How is the author organizing the book?

Some sample activities include

- Post-its: Find important passages and on the post-it, write down the analysis of the language and rhetoric. Remember to move beyond summary and main idea.
- Think-aloud: Record yourself (video or audio) reading important passages and speaking your analysis.
- Writing: Write out your important passages and the analysis, either in paragraph form or in bullet points.
- Visual: Pull important passages and find or create a visual that represents each. Include a brief explanation of your choices.

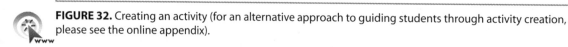

FIGURE 32. Creating an activity (for an alternative approach to guiding students through activity creation, please see the online appendix).

Phil, a sophomore, used these prompts to incorporate the following into the first activity he created on his own:

- Self-selected text: Mark Twain's *Tom Sawyer*
- EQ: Why do people get themselves into trouble?
- CCSS.ELA-Literacy.RL.9-10.5 (CCSSI, 2010): Analyze how an author's choices concerning how to structure a text, order events within it (e.g., parallel plots), and manipulate time (e.g., pacing, flashbacks) create such effects as mystery, tension, or surprise.

He chose to take a straightforward approach to his activity by selecting quotes from the text that related to his EQ. But, as you can see in Figure 33, he also then explained how the quote related to the events of the novel and how the author's choices created a specific reading experience that the reader could relate to.

"He continued pushing cautiously till he judged he might squeeze through on his knees." (133)

In this scene we see Tom trying to go and sneak back into the house without being seen since his Aunt thinks that he is gone for good. His Aunt is quite literally on her knees wishing she could have him back while Tom is crawling on the floor hiding from her. Tom does this so that this way he can go back to his home secretly while postponing judgement. I think all kids have felt this way before, after doing something bad we all want to run away from it. That is why I concluded that people trying to patch or pause their troubles just end up in more trouble. One prime example of this is lieing about your lies. We all know they are going to be exposed sometime, but we would much rather exchange our lie surfacing today for our lie surfacing tomorrow, plus some interest. Twain creates tension in the fact that he uses an event that many people have been through. By making it something that we all can relate to we all can experience it with Tom. When reading this I had felt like I was in that cautious and nervous state of Hypnosis when you are trying to be so quiet that your heart stops the second you hear a floorboard creek. Having this common foreground for the set of this story makes it much more relatable, so we go through the same stress and anxiety that Tom is going through. I truly think that Mark Twain was thinking: "just give yourself in" when Tom is trying to get away with something that is fully impossible. I mean, how can you expect to walk into your house when you have been missing and your Aunt thinks you are not alive. Its not like you can come down to breakfast the next morning and say, "I am indeed Iron Man and the Avengers had called."

FIGURE 33. Phil's reading activity.

As students gain experience with activity completion, the teacher can encourage more creative approaches to demonstrate student learning, but this first attempt at activity creation and completion does exactly what it needs to. The student pulled in the three components (text, EQ, and standard) and demonstrated skill proficiency with only guidance from his teacher.

Strategy: Adapting Existing Graphic Organizers

Pointing students toward graphic organizers can be extremely helpful as students create their own activities for the first time, especially if they are new to the language of the standard. We often do mini-lessons using graphic organizers, which students can then adapt for any reading standard. Some of the graphic organizers we have used include TPCASTT (title–paraphrase–connotation–attitude–shifts–

Pitfall: When Individualization Isolates Students from One Another

One of the beautiful outcomes of getting students more involved in standards is that lesson planning becomes a collaborative experience between teacher and student, and also among students. However, this wasn't the case when Cathy and Heather attempted to individualize the learning of American literature students for the first time. As they pushed students toward more independence, they realized that it was isolating them from one another. Therefore, we incorporated inquiry circles (see Chapter 4). Without them, students were not gaining important collaboration skills, couldn't learn from one another, and simply felt alone in their pursuits. We use grouping not only to explore texts or questions, but also to work on standards. Students may have an initial group that focuses on a question, and then branch out into other groups to receive support from those who are working on the same standard. However, they periodically return to their original group to continue their work on their question exploration.

title–theme), SOAPSTone (speaker–occasion–audience–purpose–subject–tone), DUCATS (diction–unity–coherence–audience–tone–syntax), and DIDLS (diction–imagery–details–language–sentence structure). Students can then adapt these well-established tools for their own needs, as seen in Figure 34. After a mini-lesson on how to analyze a painting, Kyle, a sophomore, combined elements of art criticism with graphic organizers to create his own, which he named "C-SPLATT."

Painting: American Progress by John Gast (1872)

Analysis Parts: Acronym: C-SPLATT

Colors: What are the main and secondary colors, and what effect does it create in the painting? How are they painted on the canvas? Is there contrasting in the painting?

Standouts: What (if there are) objects in the painting stand out more than others? What is their significance?

People: Are there people in the painting? Who are they and where are they from? Are they significant in history?

Location: Where is the painting taking place? Is it in one specific spot or a general location?

Actions: What is going on in the painting? Are there objects in action or in standstill?

Time: What timeframe is it in? What time of year and time of day? When was it painted? Was there a significant part of history happening?

Theme: What is the general theme that the painter wants to create? Are there emotions that are more prevalent than others? What should the viewer take away?

FIGURE 34. Kyle's C-SPLATT graphic organizer.

Pitfall: When Activities Lack Creativity

There are many reasons why students choose to take the "safe" route with their activity design, but, as we explained in the introduction, we want our students to take risks and design activities that reflect their learning process. This is especially important to us for the reading activities. Unlike writing and speaking standards, for which students are required to write and speak, reading proficiency can be demonstrated in many, many ways, yet our students often want to rely on writing and speaking to explain what and how they read. When we see students getting into a rut in activity design, we introduce them to Howard Gardner's (n.d.) concept of multiple intelligences, explaining that, not only can we learn in different ways, but we can also express that learning in different fashions.

We developed a series of questions to help students respond to a text with verbal/linguistic skills, the mode most often exercised in English classes:

- How can you communicate a main idea or message from the text through writing or speaking?

- What format would be most effective to extend or build upon the ideas of the text?

- How might the language you use reflect the language of the piece? How or why would it vary?

- How would you alter the words you use for different audiences?

We then adapted these questions for visual/spatial, bodily/kinesthetic, intrapersonal, interpersonal, logical/mathematical, naturalistic, and musical intelligences. Figure 35 features different questions you can use to inspire more creative approaches to activity design.

Asking students to stretch beyond writing and speaking to demonstrate their learning provides them with a lot of possibilities. Those who are natural musicians might compose a song to demonstrate the way two characters interact, while students who are more prone to logical/mathematical thinking might be able to chart the progress of an argument. This freedom gives students a chance to demonstrate their growth and understanding in ways that are potentially more creative, more comprehensive, and more suitable to the topic and audience.

continued on next page

1. **Visual/Spatial**—Involves visual perception of the environment, the ability to create and manipulate mental images, and the orientation of the body in space.
    1. How can you communicate a main idea or message from the text visually or spatially?
    2. What format would be most effective to extend or build upon the ideas of the text?
    3. How might the orientation of objects you use reflect the text? How or why would it vary?
    4. What aspect of the visual might you change for a different audience?
    5. Examples: Painting, sculpture, photo essay, maze
2. **Bodily/Kinesthetic**—Involves physical coordination and dexterity, using fine and gross motor skills, and expressing oneself or learning through physical activities.
    1. How can you communicate a main idea or message from the text through physical movement?
    2. What format would be most effective to extend or build upon the ideas of the text?
    3. How might the movements you use reflect the text? How or why would it vary?
    4. How would you alter the movements you use for different audiences?
    5. Examples: Dance, tableau, charades, pantomime, puppet show, cake decorating
3. **Interpersonal**—Involves understanding how to communicate with and understand other people and how to work collaboratively.
    1. How can you communicate a main idea or message from the text through interpersonal relationships—you and your audience or you and your groupmates?
    2. What format would be most effective to extend or build upon the ideas of the dance?
    3. How might your group collaboration or relationship with the audience reflect the text? How or why would it vary?
    4. How would you alter your communication for different audiences?
    5. Examples: Bulletin board, advertisement, interview, writing a new law
4. **Intrapersonal**—Involves understanding one's inner world of emotions and thoughts, and growing in the ability to control them and work with them consciously.
    1. How can you communicate a main idea or message from the text through writing or speaking?
    2. What format would be most effective to extend or build upon the ideas of the text?
    3. How might the emotions/thoughts you experience reflect the text? How or why would it vary?
    4. How could you experience your emotions/thoughts in the presence of different audiences? Ex. I can't burst into tears every time I feel sad, but I might express it or experience it in ways that are appropriate for my current environment.
    5. How does your perception (beliefs, values, attitudes) of the world impact your demonstration of the document's message?
    6. Examples: Diary/journal entry, meditation, drawing emotions/parts
5. **Naturalist**—Involves understanding the natural world of plants and animals, noticing their characteristics, and categorizing them; it generally involves keen observation and the ability to classify other things as well.
    1. How can you communicate a main idea or message from the text through connecting to nature?
    2. What organization would be most effective to extend or build upon the ideas of the text?
    3. How might your classification, observations, or structure reflect the message of the text? How or why would it vary?
    4. How would you alter the relationships or classifications you use for different audiences?
    5. Examples: Scientific drawing, walkabout, evidence collection and categorization,
6. **Logical/Mathematical**—Involves number and computing skills, recognizing patterns and relationships, timeliness and order, and the ability to solve different kinds of problems through logic.
    1. How can you communicate a main idea or message from the text through using numbers, computing, patterns, organization, etc.?
    2. What format and organization would be most effective to extend or build upon the ideas of the text?
    3. How might the relationship between the components you design reflect the components of the text? How or why would it vary?
    4. How would you alter the order or organization you use for different audiences?
    5. Examples: Character growth, timeline, graphic organizer, computer program,
7. **Musical**—Involves understanding and expressing oneself through music and rhythmic movements or dance, or composing, playing, or conducting music.
    1. How can you communicate a main idea or message from the text through music?
    2. What genre of music would be most effective to extend or build upon the ideas of the text?
    3. How might the musical components (lyrics, dynamics, pace, etc.) you use reflect the text? How or why would it vary?
    4. How would you alter the musical components you use for different audiences?
    5. Example: write a song/lyrical poem, compose a musical score

FIGURE 35. Multiple intelligences activity prompts. Adapted from Gardner (n.d.).

Strategy: Building a Database of Activity Ideas

Just as we build a database of rubrics, we also collect activity ideas. We use a Google Doc where students can contribute and look up types of activities that would fulfill their chosen standards. Figure 36 shows an excerpt from one of our activity "databases." If there isn't access to an online space, students could still share their ideas for an activity. Something as simple as strategy ideas on sticky notes around the room can be the catalyst for an effective activity. Creating an "activity bank" helps build students' collaborative spirit and confidence. When students find success, they're usually excited to share it.

Speaking and Listening (from the Common Core State Standards)

3. Evaluate a speaker's point of view, reasoning, and use of evidence and rhetoric, assessing the stance, premises, links among ideas, word choice, points of emphasis, and tone used.

- Watch a YouTube video of a reading of a short text (there are MANY online!) and create a chart in which you evaluate (judge) the effectiveness of the reading by the criteria listed in the standard. Consider the speaker's choices and their effects on you as the listener.
- Listen to a small group discussion about your topic (if there is one), and evaluate one person's point of view, reasoning, and evidence by the criteria in the standard. Consider the speaker's choices and their effects on the other people in the group.

4. Present information, findings, and supporting evidence, conveying a clear and distinct perspective, such that listeners can follow the line of reasoning, alternative or opposing perspectives are addressed, and the organization, development, substance, and style are appropriate to purpose, audience, and a range of formal and informal tasks.

- Have a small group discussion in which you present information from your book to support your ideas about its themes, characters, style, and plot.
- Consider who would most benefit from reading or viewing one of your texts and present a cogent, convincing argument to that person or group to read it.

5. Make strategic use of digital media (e.g., textual, graphical, audio, visual, and interactive elements) in presentations to enhance understanding of findings, reasoning, and evidence and to add interest.

- Make a video trailer for your book. Include digital media to entice the viewer without giving away too many key elements of the plot. Instead, hype up its dynamic characters and themes by using various types of media to highlight its interesting elements that most readily connect to your peers' experiences. For a smaller text, do a book talk for the class to share what you're reading. Incorporate reasons why someone might want to read it like its connections to specific themes, questions, skills, etc. This might be something that you do over a couple of speaking activities—the first being a draft of the presentation and the second being the presentation itself.
- Present about your theme to the class or another audience. Use multimedia to engage your audience and enhance your most important points. This might be something that you do over a couple of speaking activities—the first being a draft of the presentation and the second being the presentation itself.

FIGURE 36. Speaking and listening activity database. CCSS excerpted from CCSSI (2010).

Strategy: Combining Standards to Incorporate Language Skills

Another strategy is to help students see how they can combine multiple standards into a single activity. Because we prefer not to assess language skills out of context, we often suggest that they be combined with either writing or reading standards. Doing so replaces the need for out-of-context exercises about punctuation or vocabulary. By combining a language standard with another skill area, students get to apply language skills to their own reading comprehension or their own writing. For instance, Jenna, a tenth-grade student, combined standard CCSS.ELA-Literacy.RL.9-10.1:

> Cite strong and thorough textual evidence to support analysis of what the text says explicitly as well as inferences drawn from the text. (CCSSI, 2010)

with standard CCSS.ELA-Literacy.L.9-10.3:

> Apply knowledge of language to understand how language functions in different contexts, to make effective choices for meaning or style, and to comprehend more fully when reading or listening. (CCSSI, 2010)

Her resulting activity idea was to create a Prezi (see https://prezi.com/) that compared and contrasted authors' arguments about bullying. Specifically, she examined the language surrounding incidents of bullying in three different texts and determined the impact of each author's words (see Figure 37). When students combine standards, they get to see how reading, writing, speaking, and other skills impact one another.

Strategy: Tackling the More Complex Standards

When it comes to some of the more intense standards, we like to break them into parts that can be tackled more easily. This allows the student to complete that objective over the course of different activities, focusing on one skill at a time, rather than focusing on a combination of them. For example, standard CCSS.ELA-LITERACY.RI.9-10.2 states:

> Determine a central idea of a text and analyze its development over the course of the text, including how it emerges and is shaped and refined by specific details; provide an objective summary of the text. (CCSSI, 2010)

Transcript of Comparing Arguments among Different Texts

In each of the following texts, the authors make arguments about bullying. I will try to answer my essential question by analyzing the different arguments made, analyzing the style of writing that helped me conclude this, and analyzing textual evidence.

The Essential Question: How does bullying affect another person?

Text 1:
Thirteen Reasons Why by Jay Asher is a book about a girl named Hannah Baker who has a series of events in her life that eventually lead to suicide. Before she killed herself, Hannah recorded 13 tapes recalling the 13 events that primarily caused Hannah to commit suicide. Most of the events were centered on bullying.

Example 1:
As part of Hannah's peer communications class, the students must leave strips of paper with compliments on them for their classmates. Hannah notices that her bag is constantly empty, and she soon catches fellow classmate Zach stealing her bag. She assumes that this is revenge because she had ignored him at the local restaurant the other day. Hannah describes her frustration with Zach by saying, "Maybe it didn't seem like a big deal to you, Zach. But now, I hope you understand. My world was collapsing. I needed those notes. I needed any hope those notes might have offered. And you? You took that hope away. You decided I didn't deserve to have it" (Asher 165).

Connection to Plot
This sentence adds to the plot by showing the point in time in which Hannah loses one of her only sources of positivity, as well as all hope. This causes her to become even more depressed.

The Author's Craft
The way an author presents information to you can help determine its meaning. For example, the author chose to have Hannah tell Zach what he did wrong, but instead of immediately confronting him, she waits until she had already made the decision to commit suicide. This shows that Hannah had very little confidence and therefore could not stand up for herself when she was being bullied. However, this also shows a little bit of Hannah's immaturity. One can understand why it would be difficult for Hannah to confront someone who bullied her, but it would have been much easier for her to reach out to a teacher, guidance counselor, or parent. This way, she could have gotten help and possibly prevented suicide. In addition, Asher chooses to include many accusatory phrases in Hannah's language. Hannah shows how she was victimized by Zach by saying, "You took that hope away. You decided I didn't deserve to have it" (Asher 165). This kind of language was used to portray Hannah's innocence and Asher wants the reader to sympathize with Hannah. In reality, if she hadn't ignored Zach at the restaurant, the incident could have been avoided all together. Zach's bullying wasn't completely spontaneous; it was the result of one of Hannah's actions. Additionally, reaching out for help could have prevented suicide.

Another way that the author presents information is through the sentence structure and grammar within the sentences. For instance, in the quote from example 1, Asher uses many simple sentences to easily get Hannah's point across to Zach. Also, Asher switches off using Hannah and Zach as subjects of the sentences to convey the meaning that he wants. When he wants to show how Zach affected Hannah, he makes Hannah the subject. This allows him to express her inner thoughts and feelings about being bullied. When Asher wants Hannah to confront Zach about his actions, Zach becomes the subject. This allows Hannah to defend herself and accuse Zach.

Argument
After analyzing a passage of Thirteen Reasons Why, it is clear that Asher's argument is that bullying causes a person to lose confidence as well as become defensive. This can be found by analyzing how the author crafts their writing.

[Text 2 and Example 2]

Conclusion
After analyzing the arguments made about bullying from two different books, I have concluded that bullying can cause a person to lose self-confidence and become defensive. However, with an optimistic mindset, you can learn lessons from bullying at the end of the day.

FIGURE 37. Excerpts from the transcript of Jenna's Prezi (to see Jenna's full ILP for this unit, please refer to the online appendix).

By isolating the action verbs, students can break this down into three parts: (1) figuring out the main idea, (2) finding details from the text to explain how the main idea develops or evolves, and (3) providing a nonbiased summary. Each of these steps can then be practiced by the student as a separate activity before combining all three parts for a final assessment.

Strategy: Teaching Students How to Scaffold Their Own Learning

We typically ask students to think of the actions and products of these standards in terms of steps. Jenna, for example, wanted to work on improving her conclusions. For her first writing activity, she studied a student model recommended by the CCSS to see how the essay concludes and then developed a list of criteria for her own conclusions. After receiving feedback, her second activity for this skill was writing an essay introduction with a conclusion that followed her criteria. Ultimately, she wrote a full-length, processed piece showing mastery of that skill for the final activity. Suggesting this type of flexibility provides students with additional comfort with the skill's requirements before they're expected to complete a polished piece in a single activity. Like traditional classes, our writing processes are scaffolded. The biggest difference is that, with this type of practice, students are designing their own scaffolded steps for writing as well as reading, speaking, and listening. To see Jenna's steps toward mastery, please refer to her full ILP in the online appendix.

Strategy: Developing Unique, Skill-Based Goals That Go beyond the Standards

Periodically, students and teachers will recognize needs that are not covered by any established standard. When that happens, we encourage students to develop their own goals. This provides an opportunity for students to do things like examine artwork or write poetry. Neither skill is highlighted in the CCSS, yet they are intriguing and challenging for many students.

Sam, a senior, developed the following standard for himself: "Examine the effectiveness of varied writing processes (e.g., working conditions, using memory aids to remember details of an experience before writing about it) by experimenting in my writing process." His activities that incorporated this standard included analyzing the writing processes of established writers, as well as developing and testing various strategies for his own process. These experiments then helped him answer his EQ, "What does writing do for the creator?" Because of his prior work with the standards, Sam was able to craft his own in an area not explicitly covered by the CCSS.

III

Letting Go of the Grader

Entrusting Students with Charting Their Own Progress

In her piece "Willing to Be Disturbed," Wheatley (2002) stated that:

> We weren't trained to admit we don't know. Most of us were taught to sound certain and confident, to state our opinion as if it were true. We haven't been rewarded for being confused. Or for asking more questions rather than giving quick answers. (p. 34)

This "training" likely starts in school. In the same breath that we lament students' lack of desire to take risks, we announce another exam for which knowing the answers is the only assessment criteria, rewarding students who get it right the first time while maybe giving half-credit to those who do corrections. Of course, assessment of knowledge is important in school, but, as Wheatley's admission reminds us, we need to engender something even more important: a "willingness to be disturbed," which can only come when students feel the freedom to make mistakes and see them as opportunities for learning. We really can't blame students for being risk averse when they live in systems of schooling that focus on summative assessment and ranking. In his article "From Degrading to De-Grading," Kohn (2004) described this phenomenon as follows:

> The more pressure to get an A, the less inclination to truly challenge oneself. Thus, students who cut corners may not be lazy so much as rational; they are adapting to an environment where good grades, not intellectual exploration, are what count. (p. 76)

Coupled with a view of high school as simply a hurdle rather than a learning experience, this pressure to get an A also creates a desire to be told what to learn; however, this mindset will not serve students well in the future. Of course, college is important, but, if school is only about the next hurdle or reward and not about the learning itself, we risk stunting a student's intrinsic desire to learn. Given the chance, students see this too. Nolan, a junior, demonstrated this in a video he created for his British Literature class:

> Up until I started the inquiry process, I saw learning as purely academic, with no relative meaning to my own life, but [my final product] will show how wrong I was and the positive outcome I got out of the class. I wish to show this to the administration to prove that students are amazing individuals and not just grades on a sheet. The movie will be creative, it will show my progression and my reasons are to show that no good can come out of being lazy. You have to struggle, you have to have times of doubt in order to find yourself. See you on the other side!

The ILP process encourages us to rethink assessment to better capture student growth, allow for risk-taking, and be more meaningful for students.

Types of Assessments

To provide a comprehensive look at a student, we need to think carefully about what warrants summative assessment and to use these along with other types of assessments. Martin-Kniep and Picone-Zocchia (2009) provided a detailed explanation for using assessment:

> Truly assessing students' learning means measuring how they can use and share what they know, what and how they think about learning and about themselves as learners, how they process and use information, and what they can create by combining what they have learned with available resources. It means finding opportunities to discern how students transfer what they have learned in one context to a different one, how they express what they have read or know to different audiences, how they react under pressure, and how well they can answer and ask questions. (pp. 66–67)

With all of this to assess, it should be no surprise that we need far more than just summative assessments, particularly those that focus on the measurement of remembered facts, which is why we use three additional types, as detailed next.

Diagnostic Assessments

In Chapter 4, we discussed using diagnostic assessments to help students select individual focus standards for us to understand where students are when they arrive in our classes. Martin-Kniep and Picone-Zocchia (2009) described diagnostic assessment as:

> . . . a glimpse of where students are relative to what is about to be taught and providing the opportunity to make early adjustments or rethink upcoming learning opportunities by keeping in mind the students who are about to engage in them. (p. 70)

Therefore, we begin our units with these types of assessments in the major skill areas. For most of our English courses, those skills are reading, writing, and speaking and listening, in accordance with the breakdown of the CCSS. Not only do the diagnostics gauge a starting point and help us adjust, but they also help to uncover student strengths and weaknesses so learning can be individualized.

Formative Assessments

We make sure our courses are full of this type of feedback. As mentioned in Chapter 5, students go through multiple sequences, or rounds, of formative activities without fear of punitive grading. Martin-Kniep and Picone-Zocchia (2009) shared the significant potential of using formative assessments, as well as some examples of how they can be implemented:

> Timed well, they can reveal issues of misunderstanding or confusion before they become obstacles to student learning. Formative assessments are planned and documented (e.g., conferences, observations, review of work or proposed goals, and strategic plans); they aim to provide information about student progress, in progress. They don't generate formal grades but are rich in the feedback they provide. (p. 73)

This type of assessment has increased students' willingness to take risks and grow as learners. For example, Erin, a senior, explained the benefit of being assessed formatively this way:

> Regarding the structure of this course I really like how it sets you up for success. I enjoy being able to have two attempts before the final copy....I knew what I had to do by the time the third group of activities came around to receive the grade I wanted.

Self-Assessments

The last type of assessment is one often taken for granted by teachers. Many of us don't remember how we learned to self-assess and, therefore, may have inflated expectations for our students' abilities to assess themselves effectively and at appropriate times. Some studies have indicated that this expectation may not be valid: "The ability to be aware of and reflect on one's own process while undertaking to learn develops late in children, and it does not automatically increase with age" (Martin-Kniep & Picone-Zocchia, 2009, p. 157). The ILP was created to increase the ability to self-assess, which, as Martin-Kniep and Picone-Zocchia (2009) noted, "enables [students] to develop a deep understanding of their strengths and weaknesses and empowers them to know how to improve their work" (p. 160).

Along with summative and peer assessment, these three types of assessment are used in conjunction to provide a feedback loop between students and us, as well as with their peers. This loop provides ample practice and mentoring before any summative grades are given.

Fighting Frustration and Finding the Sweet Zone

Kuhlthau's (2004) work with the ISP detailed the importance of finding "zones of intervention" in the research process:

> The zone of intervention is that area in which an information user can do with advice and assistance what he or she cannot do alone or can do only with difficulty. . . . Intervention outside this zone is inefficient and unnecessary, experienced by users as intrusive on the one hand and as overwhelming on the other. (p. 129)

This is not just true for research. When we do any activity with students all at the same time, we may miss some students because they know it and others because they were not ready for it. To intervene, however, we need to know where students are. Process models like the ISP provide guidance, as does an ample use of reflection and formative assessment. Smith et al. (2014) addressed this idea too. One of the key concepts they explained is why it's so important to "hit the sweet spot" as students are learning, particularly when asking them to take risks: "Once students begin to struggle and enter into what Jeff [Wilhelm] calls their ZFD (zone of frustrational development), the jig is up" (p. 42).

Being challenged while learning is important, but, if we are consistently pushing students too far beyond the point of frustration and confusion, learning ceases. Put another way:

> Just as we put up a scaffold to support and structure the construction of a wall or building, we must do the same for students as they are learning new concepts and strategies. Just as the scaffolding is taken away when the building can stand on its own, we do the same in our teaching. (Smith et al., 2014, p. 64)

Based on these theories, the ILP process includes multiple opportunities for reflection as students learn, chances to practice each skill or standard multiple times before receiving a grade, and opportunities to work one on one with us and with small groups of peers who are also working on the same learning goals.

6

Strategies for Assessment, Feedback, and Conferencing

We make sure that students understand the important relationship between the types of assessment discussed previously. In Chapter 4, we explained how diagnostics set the stage for the class so that students can determine which skills they need to improve on, but the most growth comes during the formative stage of this process. We use a variety of strategies to give students the tools to grow and reflect on their learning.

Assessment in Action

Formative assessment is built into the process through rounds of activities. We also provide opportunities for self-assessment and the identification of strengths and areas for growth. In addition to traditional assessment tools like rubrics, we create flowcharts to help students begin to assess their progress.

Strategy: Completing Rounds of Activities

We explain to students that the purpose of the activities is to practice skills, get feedback on their work, and improve throughout the unit to reach the requirements of "Proficient" or "Advanced proficient." This is why the ILP builds in multiple opportunities for practice by completing more than one formative activity for each skill. This creates a feedback loop, allowing students to return to a skill multiple times while also allowing you to formatively assess their work.

Usually, the ILP provides students with two formative attempts at each skill before they receive a final grade. We call these formative attempts "rounds," and, at the end of each round, students have the chance to pause, assess their progress, and set goals for the upcoming round. As one tenth-grade student, Mark, wrote, "There's really a huge difference between 'Oh, I'll do better next time' and 'This is what I'll do differently next time.'" This combination of practice and reflection allows students to articulate their own learning needs and assess their work more accurately. (We explore strategies for reflection in Chapter 7.)

What Does This Look Like in a Gradebook?

In Meg's and Cathy's classes, formative grades do not get averaged into the course grade. Instead, only summative grades, which usually come at the end of the unit, get averaged in. This can leave some students confused as to where they stand in the class, so it is important that they have a clear record of their performance on all types of assessments. This can be done by inputting unweighted grades for formative assessments into an online gradebook or by having students keep a record of their grades when they receive their assignments back (see Figure 38).

Assignment Name	Strengths	Weaknesses	On-time	Score

FIGURE 38. Grade log.

Represented in the gradebook example in Figure 39 are the second and third attempts at each of the following skills: reading, writing, and speaking/listening skills. The first and second attempts were assessed formatively, and thus are categorized as, for example, "RF," denoting a reading assessment that was formative. Since "Reading 3" was the third and final activity of the unit for that skill, it is the summative reading grade, noted not only by the number "3" but also by the category of "Reading" as opposed to "RF." Figure 39 carries this process through for both the writing and speaking/listening grades, so, in this example, the student would see three formative grades followed by three summative grades. Furthermore, in this gradebook, any formative grade category is *unweighted*, meaning that it does not make up a percentage of the final grade, whereas the summative categories do make up a certain percentage of the final course grade. For some teachers, having formative categories that are entirely unweighted is not an option, so they may want to count formative assignments for fewer points than summative, such as five points versus a hundred.

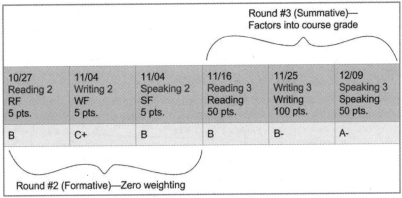

FIGURE 39. Gradebook example.

Pitfall: When a Summative Assessment Is Worse Than a Formative One

Ideally, a student will show improvement from one round to the next, but, when they haven't, it is often because they took a big risk with a final activity. That is, the shifts that the student made improved certain parts of the skill, but other aspects suffered. When the grade does not improve, we give them additional feedback, commend them for taking a new risk, and keep the higher formative grade as their summative score (this was the case for the example shown in Figure 39). We want students to know that they won't be penalized for trying something new since they have previously demonstrated a higher proficiency of the skill.

Strategy: Self-Assessment Using the Standards and Rubrics

Though most of these strategies can be used separately, for students to self-assess, they need to utilize the strategy for a "close-reading of the standards" found in Chapter 4. Without the foundation that doing a close-read provides, students will not have the understanding to accurately self-assess. In addition to the close-reads, students also have teacher- or student-created rubrics to use for self-assessment. We always tell our students to use the rubrics like a checklist, marking off what they have completed in their activity with reference to the "Developing," "Proficient," and "Advanced proficient" ranges. Whether they are assessing their work in the middle of an activity or at the end of it, students should be sure to determine what they are missing that is preventing them from improving.

Pitfall: When Self-Assessment Attacks

Students may not correctly assess themselves all the time. We have had some moments when we've looked at a rubric and realized there is a disconnect between the student's self-assessment and their actual skill level. We've also had students who have described their work as "Proficient" when they have rocked "Advanced proficient"! When this happens, it's time to reboot and go back to the standard and the rubric with the student individually.

Regarding students who think they have done much better than they actually did, this usually means they don't understand the rubric and what is being asked of them. Even when students helped to create the rubric in a small group, they might need more clarification about a specific word or phrase. If the rubric relies on that knowledge, students might struggle to reach proficiency. For example, one sophomore, Karl, recently struggled with the phrase "break down the process" that his group members had used in the rubric to describe the word *analyze*. As a result, Meg had the group create a list of items they should "break down" when analyzing the story. This allowed Karl to move from barely "Developing" to "Proficient" in one round of activities.

Conversely, when students score their work lower than it should be, this usually is not a misinterpretation of the rubric, but, rather, a lack of confidence in their skills. When pressed for evidence, these students usually cannot provide any for why they are not "Advanced proficient." Instead, some of these students simply don't believe that they are "A students" or they are afraid of being seen as conceited. Therefore, it is important for you and the student to have a one-on-one discussion to review the specifications of the rubric. In all matters of self-assessment, students must look at their work objectively, as though someone else were assessing it. This way, the conversation can become an explanation of the importance of celebrating one's accomplishments.

Strategy: Identifying Strengths and Needs

Assessing more than a hundred activities is a daunting task, especially when students rely on our feedback in order to improve before a summative assessment, and a quick turnaround is important. One way we can cut back on our time spent assessing activities and encourage students to become more self-aware of what they have accomplished is by having them annotate their activity before they submit it (see Figure 40). Students break down the standard or the rubric into its basic elements and then identify where in the activity is their best attempt at the skill. This allows students to recognize their strengths, but it also makes them cognizant of their weaknesses. If they are unable to identify the application of a standard in their work, then that pinpoints a clear need for them. It can also be helpful to have students rank their examples, so, if they have identified three areas in the activity where they have practiced the standard, they can show you what they are most proud of and what they think they still need help on.

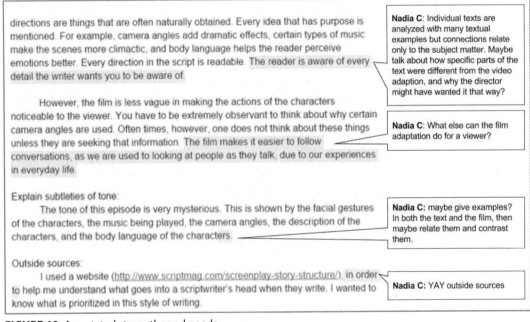

directions are things that are often naturally obtained. Every idea that has purpose is mentioned. For example, camera angles add dramatic effects, certain types of music make the scenes more climactic, and body language helps the reader perceive emotions better. Every direction in the script is readable. The reader is aware of every detail the writer wants you to be aware of.

> **Nadia C:** Individual texts are analyzed with many textual examples but connections relate only to the subject matter. Maybe talk about how specific parts of the text were different from the video adaption, and why the director might have wanted it that way?

However, the film is less vague in making the actions of the characters noticeable to the viewer. You have to be extremely observant to think about why certain camera angles are used. Often times, however, one does not think about these things unless they are seeking that information. The film makes it easier to follow conversations, as we are used to looking at people as they talk, due to our experiences in everyday life.

> **Nadia C:** What else can the film adaptation do for a viewer?

Explain subtleties of tone:
The tone of this episode is very mysterious. This is shown by the facial gestures of the characters, the music being played, the camera angles, the description of the characters, and the body language of the characters.

> **Nadia C:** maybe give examples? In both the text and the film, then maybe relate them and contrast them.

Outside sources:
I used a website (http://www.scriptmag.com/screenplay-story-structure/), in order to help me understand what goes into a scriptwriter's head when they write. I wanted to know what is prioritized in this style of writing.

> **Nadia C:** YAY outside sources

FIGURE 40. Annotated strengths and needs.

Pitfall: When a Student Masters a Skill Early in the Process

Each standard should be practiced at least once during each round of activities. If a skill is mastered prior to the final assessment, students can add in or move on to another skill within the same category. For example, students who show mastery of standard SL.9-10.1 during discussions can incorporate an additional standard, such as SL.9-10.2, into their future discussions:

- CCSS.ELA-Literacy.SL.9-10.1: Initiate and participate effectively in a range of collaborative discussions (one on one, in groups, and teacher-led) with diverse partners on grades 9-10 topics, texts, and issues, building on others' ideas and expressing their own clearly and persuasively.

- CCSS.ELA-Literacy.SL.9-10.2: Integrate multiple sources of information presented in diverse media or formats (e.g., visually, quantitatively, orally) evaluating the credibility and accuracy of each source. (CCSSI, 2010)

By focusing on a second standard, students add complexity to their skill work. In the preceding example, they will still need to build off others' ideas and express their own thoughts, but they will have the additional element of incorporating more multimedia sources into that discussion. Moreover, they will have to "evaluate the credibility and accuracy of each source." One class decided that should mean "show[ing] multiple sides to a topic" by "examin[ing] claims and counterclaims" that the sources make. Therefore, students might also decide to examine the credibility of their peers' sources in discussions. When applied to the existing requirements from SL.9-10.1, this second standard makes small-group discussion much more challenging and sophisticated.

Another option for students who have mastered a reading or listening skill is to attempt the same skill but with more challenging texts. This allows the student to continue working alongside peers as well as using the same rubric for each activity.

Strategy: Using Flowcharts

Flowcharts help students identify their strengths and needs and move easily through the process of self-assessment. In Meg's final unit for sophomore English, students study poetry, satire, and extended definitions. They work with each mode of writing by reading models and creating lists of "must haves" for each type of writing. They then use these lists to create flowcharts, such as the one shown in Figure 41. Students use these as a checklist of sorts for their writing, striving to reach "Advanced proficient" before turning in their assignment.

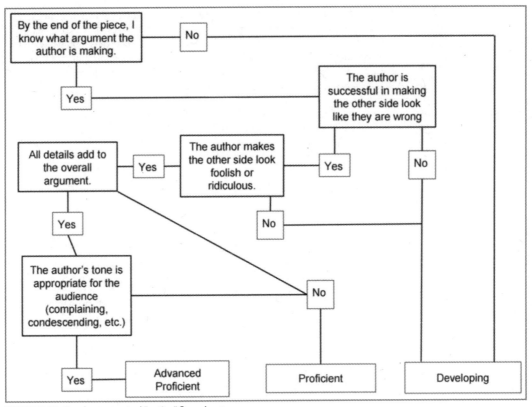

FIGURE 41. Student-created "satire" flowchart.

Pitfall: Focusing on the Grade Instead of the Learning

In today's high-stakes educational environment, students often get caught up in what their grade is rather than whether they are learning and developing as readers, writers, and speakers. Some students want to complete an assignment only if they know they are receiving a summative grade. We often hear the refrain, "Does this count?" It *all* counts! We make sure to show these students the connection between the formative and summative activities, so that, when they complete the formative activities and follow the feedback they have received, they *will* improve on the next attempt. There are also students who, when they see that C (or D or F) for a formative assignment, go into panic mode. Parents can also fall into this worry-trap. Again, we reiterate to both parents and students that this is practice and that they will succeed on the next round if they apply the feedback they are given.

We also make sure to celebrate the achievement of changing habits. When students can practice before they receive a grade, they are more likely to take risks in their work; we tend to see more thinking and wondering in formative activities than we would if the assignment were to receive a grade. For example, the following statements, overheard during a formative scored discussion on Tim O'Brien's "Spin" from *The Things They Carried*, demonstrate a "willingness to be disturbed":

> STUDENT A: There is a quote on the second to last page … (*reads quote*). I am confused as to what the author meant.
>
> […]
>
> STUDENT A: Why does it say …?
>
> STUDENT B: I don't know—he probably doesn't remember how it started…
>
> STUDENT C: But also it was something so traumatic….
>
> […]
>
> STUDENT A: I found it confusing the entire time.
>
> STUDENT B: Yeah, there were fifteen people and they kept coming in….
>
> […]
>
> STUDENT A: I have a question—does anybody have any idea what the title means?
>
> STUDENT B: It says on the first page, it says … which also goes back to his point of view…. I say it is good for him … it is like putting a spin on it … so maybe that is why it is called "Spin."
>
> […]
>
> STUDENT C: Does anybody know what the theme is?
>
> STUDENT A: It is hard because this is an excerpt but I would say…

Students feel comfortable voicing their confusion with one another, and they feel confident that they can learn from one another. It's important to establish that culture for learning through the celebration of risk-taking and the emphasis on growth from feedback.

Using Feedback for Individualized Growth

Feedback from peers, teachers, and experts can be invaluable. Reading, writing, and speaking activities are meant to convey students' understanding to someone outside of their own heads. By asking someone else to review their work, students can receive important information about their abilities, which can help them articulate what they know and how they know it in later self-assessments. Often, we think of feedback as the domain of teachers because they are the experts in the room; however, peer feedback is just as crucial. Peers may have a fledgling grasp of the skills, so they typically ask more genuine questions, whereas we are often tempted to provide answers based on our experience and expertise. Critiquing a peer's work also gives reviewers practice in examining the skill's requirements and provides an opportunity to see how their fellow classmates are working through their own uncertainties. Afterwards, we may point students toward specific strategies with which to improve or provide feedback that pushes them to move beyond proficiency.

Strategy: Using Teacher-Created Peer Review Questions

If all students are working on the same standard, we use a peer review sheet to focus students on the language of the rubric and standard being practiced. Following is an example of a peer review sheet for standards CCSS.ELA-Literacy.W.11-12.1.a-b (CCSSI, 2010):

- a: Introduce precise, knowledgeable claim(s), establish the significance of the claim(s), distinguish the claim(s) from alternate or opposing claims, and create an organization that logically sequences claim(s), counterclaims, reasons, and evidence.
- b: Develop claim(s) and counterclaims fairly and thoroughly, supplying the most relevant evidence for each while pointing out the strengths and limitations of both in a manner that anticipates the audience's knowledge level, concerns, values, and possible biases.

This technique ensures that students focus on specific elements of the standard for argument writing. Cathy's peer review worksheet (see Figure 42) asks students to target the establishment and development of claims. Identifying those elements within a peer's text can give important insights to the writer and to the peer reviewer. If it's difficult for peers to find a claim, for example, or if they identify something that was not intended, this practice can help students clarify their claims.

Strategy: Using Student-Created Peer Review Questions

If students have chosen unique standards and a class needs multiple peer review sheets, ask students to develop questions about their peers' work. This is especially useful if students have already analyzed standards and/or created rubrics for the standards as they will have an intimate understanding of what's required. In Cathy's sophomore class, she asked students to focus on a single

Annotating Peer Arguments		
Element of Argument	Text Support—Give a specific example from the argument.	Peer Notes—Explain what the writer does well, and explain in which ways the writer needs to improve.
Claim What is the author arguing?		
Reasons Why does the author think we should buy into his/her argument?		
Evidence Give examples for one of the reasons. What support does the author give for his/her reasons?		
Counterclaims What opposing argument(s) does the author introduce?		
Refutation What reason does the author provide to challenge or invalidate the counterclaim? What evidence does he/she use to support it?		

FIGURE 42. Teacher-created peer review sheet for standards CCSS.ELA-Literacy.W.11-12.1.a-b. CCSS excerpted from CCSSI (2010).

skill that they had practiced and made them the "experts" of those skills in small groups. They then revisited the language of the standard, read models of work that demonstrated that skill, and articulated criteria for surpassing the standard's requirements. Finally, they put together a list of questions they might ask themselves about the standard's criteria if they were to evaluate for that aspect of the skill. Cathy then put those questions into a single document for the entire class to use as their peer review worksheet (see Figure 43).

C. Use words, phrases, and clauses to link the major sections of the text, create cohesion, and clarify the relationships between claim(s) and reasons, between reasons and evidence, and between claim(s) and counterclaims.

Peer Review Questions:

1. Does the writer properly use transitions to connect phrases in his paragraphs?
2. Does the writer properly introduce evidence in his paragraphs?
3. Does the overall organization of the text contribute to the logical progression of ideas?
4. Does the piece include appropriate transitional phrases? (Using transitions relating to contrast, causation, etc. when needed)
5. Does the writer express a clear and consistent argument through the piece?

FIGURE 43. Student-created peer review for standard CCSS.ELA-Literacy.W.9-10.1.c. CCSS excerpted from CCSSI (2010).

Strategy: Reading Peers' Work Out Loud

Another strategy is to have students read their papers aloud to each other. Hearing their own words read by someone else is a great way for students to step back from their ideas and assess them objectively. They also use the points at which the reader stumbles over wording to identify areas that don't "read well" or need clarity. The authors will note areas in need of clarification and/or transitions as well as areas where their intention does not come through in the work. Every time the reader stops, every time the reader has questions, and every time the author doesn't hear the explanation that exists in her head, the author marks this down as an area for improvement. Meg has used audio recordings in the same way, which is an option if class time isn't available for the activity and if students have access to recording technology. Students recorded their peers' argument speeches for homework and then listened to their peers' readings the following evening before using the feedback to make revisions.

Pitfall: Not Wanting to Offend a Peer

Many times, students struggle with peer review because they are critiquing their friends and classmates. To thwart this mode of thinking, we set up a supportive atmosphere in which students focus on progress in skill criteria. We ensure that students provide feedback that will help a peer grow and improve because telling a friend that his work is "good" does nothing to help him except maybe boost an ego. When students do not provide specific positive feedback, it suggests that creating something "good" requires a natural talent rather than work and refinement. Requiring students to focus on the nuances of the skills or standards helps them look for specific criteria and then evaluate how well their peers execute those skills. When referring back to elements of the rubric and comparing to model texts, peer reviewers should be able to justify their feedback, both warm (kudos) and cool (suggestions for improvement).

If you instruct multiple sections of the same course, students can also provide peer feedback across classes. Especially when given anonymously, students are much less likely to hand back an activity and just say, "It's good."

Strategy: Receiving Expert Feedback

Since one teacher only has so much expertise, students are tasked with reaching out to writers to receive feedback on their work during the last unit of Meg's senior writing course. Because each student is studying a different type of writing, they must research and contact all sorts of experts. One student, Diane, was interested in writing obituaries, so she contacted Heather Lende, an obituary writer for *Chilkat Valley News*. Lende included her go-to structure, professional models and resources, family interview techniques, and advice about brevity, details, and mechanics that are specific to the genre. From that information, Diane developed a list of tips (see Figure 44).

Receiving this type of feedback is invaluable for students, and, if a student picks something as specific as obituary writing, then an outside expert is necessary. Meg encourages her students to think local but to make sure the person they are contacting is of literary or professional merit.

Tips on Writing Obituaries from Heather Lende:

1. Start from the beginning of the death
2. Write a little bit about what he/she did.
3. A biography
   a. Who died? What of? Where?
   b. Where and when he/she was born?
   c. His/her parents names (mother's maiden name)
   d. Schooling
   e. Service
   f. Marriages
   g. Careers
   h. Family
   i. Where he/she lived and where he/she died
4. Quotes from family or friends about him/her
   a. Encourage them to be specific
5. Details are very important.
6. Obituaries are supposed to be brief.
   a. No need to put excessive amounts of details in the obituary if it did not have a big impact on his/her life.

FIGURE 44. Obituary writing tips. Adapted with permission from Heather Lende.

Conferencing

Conferences are an essential tool in this process because they provide the type of immediate feedback that written comments can't provide. You can ask students to explain how they will improve their work, ensuring student understanding. Conferences also create a dialogue between you and your students, so you can clearly see the effect of your feedback, and adjust it if necessary. Additionally, they help to build relationships with students. Burke (2010) recommended conferring for the following important reason:

> Students who are guided by questions need help learning how to steer their way through such uncharted waters. Without guidance and accountability, students can wander from the topic they are investigating, arriving at the final with little more than a summary or an extended digression. (p. 40)

Using conferences as part of the learning process is one of the best ways to help students in these "uncharted waters." Comments on papers can be misinterpreted by both teachers and students and can't provide the give and take of ideas that conferring does.

Conferences can occur throughout the process but are often the result of a "cry for help" found in reflections. They also may stem from the tools that we create specifically to capture what students need, like the "text assistance request" form (Figure 9) and the "teacher conference request" form (see Figure 45). These types of conferences are prompted by a certain need, since the point of a conference is to help students build skills and guide them toward independence; therefore, it is our ability to question students, to tease out their true interests and needs, that makes a conference successful. The following conferring strategies are especially useful in relation to the ILP.

Strategy: Teacher Conference Requests—Formal and Informal

Often, a student may need feedback when they are completing their first formative assessment. Most of these requests for help are done informally as students come up to us with questions or needs. Because our classes are workshop based, it can be overwhelming to try to reach every student each day or even every other day. As a result, we created a Google form (see Figure 45) that allows our students to reach out to us with a specific need. This way, we are prepared ahead of time when we go to meet with the student during the next class.

Teacher Conference Request

During Unit 2, you will be much more independent. You will move through activities and reflections at a pace that is comfortable for you, and as a result, you will be responsible for letting me know when you would like a conference. If not more often, you must at least conference with me when you hit each reflection point.

Your email address (**cstutzma@hcrhs.org**) will be recorded when you submit this form. Not you? Switch account

* Required

What block do you have class? *

Your answer

What day would you prefer to conference? *
*If this date already has 5 students signed up, or if we are doing a full-class activity that day, there is a chance your conference will be pushed to the following class period.

MM   DD

___ / ___

What do you need to conference about? *

Your answer

FIGURE 45. Teacher conference request form.

Our school is very Google centered, but any survey form would work. Even a quick email or a note at the end of class would help you be prepared. Another option to request feedback for the Google-equipped is to use Google Classroom (see https://classroom.google.com). You can create individual ILPs for each student, and, when they are ready to receive feedback, they can hit "Turn in," which pushes the ILP back to you and lets you know that the student is ready to conference.

Strategy: Building Trust through Questions

A liberal use of assessment types other than just summative grading helps students to begin to take more risks. This move toward a risk-taking stance is not just a change for students, however. It requires you to try new techniques and build trust with your students. In Chapter 1, we discussed the use of student interest surveys inspired by Cushman (2010). However, these interest surveys are not only used to help students choose texts. As Cushman (2014) noted in a separate article, your interactions can go beyond these initial surveys and probe students to "tell [you] more." Cushman saw how programmed students were to finish queries about what they are very good at; they did it quickly and without much thought:

> "Tell me more," I would say. And wait, while they racked their brains for the "right answer." Sometimes, I would have to prompt their memories. ("Was it always that way for you?" "Did you ever try to teach someone how to do that?" "What's hard in getting the hang of it?") Sooner or later, they got the message: I was actually *really interested* in the details of their experience. (paras. 5–6)

Students need to feel that teachers are engaged in not just their learning but also in learning about them as people. The process of uncovering information through questions is a great way to build that connection. For example, Cathy has asked her students, "As opposed to strengths that come naturally to you, what are some skills you needed to practice in order to master?" Dennis, a tenth-grade honors student, wrote in response, "I guess that would be my violin playing. I mean, before ninth grade, I was pretty horrendous, and so I needed to practice to actually be comparable to the rest of the Freshman Orchestra." This told Cathy enough about Dennis to start a conversation. She knew he played violin and that he worked hard to match his peers' abilities. From there, she could talk with him about the practice habits he created for himself, why he felt it was important to be on the same level as the rest of the Freshman Orchestra, how he discovered the gap in his abilities, and what benefits he's seen from his increased skills and from his practice habits. This conversation easily translates into a conversation about creating habits for reading and writing.

Another student responded with only one-word descriptions of activities, school subjects, and hobbies. In this case, Cathy asked her whether riflery, one of the student's hobbies, was inherently interesting to her and why she felt motivated to practice or improve in that skill. Cathy also asked about the habits she

Managing the Workload

All of these assessments can be overwhelming, especially when you have more than one hundred students completing activities at the same time. While written feedback from a teacher is important, the following strategies, which we also detail in this chapter, can help cut down on the workload tremendously:

- *Conferencing* helps us to work through activities with students, and, when they use that as an opportunity to defend their work, it's a chance for us to assess their progress while they walk us through it.

- *Peer feedback* serves as a way for students to practice assessing work according to standards, and it also provides valuable feedback to the student even when you aren't available.

In addition to these strategies, we also do the following:

- *Staggered due dates*: This is a tried and true method for when written teacher feedback is best. We have never done this consciously, however, because the individualized nature of this process tends to stagger the submission of activities naturally.

- *Time frames for completion*: Staggering is no guarantee with the ILP process. Therefore, we reserve specific windows for providing feedback. If students do not provide completed activities in that time frame, they miss their chance at teacher feedback before the next round of activities is due.

formed in order to get better. Knowing student interests goes beyond academics. Cathy's conversations with Dennis and other students built rapport and a foundation for helping them make choices throughout the learning process. Conversations like these bring awareness to how they learn outside of class and encourage them to compare it to their in-class learning strategies.

Strategy: Conferring about Feedback: "In Defense of My Work"

Once students practice a skill and receive feedback, they can use that feedback to fuel subsequent attempts at a standard, and they can explain their work in class before submitting it for assessment. They walk through the decisions they made, how they used initial feedback to progress toward standard mastery, and how they would assess their work on the rubric (see Figure 46). This is an especially powerful strategy after students have practiced a little with a standard but before they are ready to be summatively assessed, providing them with valuable feedback and reducing your workload at home by walking through an activity with a student in class. "In defense of my work" is a crucial part of the ILP process, exemplifying the best parts of formative and self-assessment.

In Defense of My Work

This is your opportunity to explain your work and defend its assessment! Choose a reading or writing activity from this round of work. Then, during a 5-minute conference with your teacher, articulate the following:

- areas where significant progress was made, showing how work has improved from previous attempts
- areas where you can still improve with specific plans for improvement
- evidence for where your work falls on the appropriate rubric
- evidence as to how the activity helped you answer an essential question

Standard	Advanced Proficient	Proficient	Developing
CCSS.ELA-LITERACY. SL.11-12.1.A Come to discussions prepared, having read and researched material under study; explicitly draw on that preparation by referring to evidence from texts and other research on the topic or issue to stimulate a thoughtful, well-reasoned exchange of ideas.	Obviously prepared. Brings notes with references to activities from throughout the unit. Leads discussion. Accurately assesses self on reading/writing rubric.	Prepared with notes, but may not discuss scope of unit. Knowledge of activities is evident. Needs some prompting. Accurately assesses self on reading/writing rubric with some missteps.	Comes to discussion unprepared. Simplistic thinking. Needs prompting throughout conference. Inaccurate assessment of skills. Argumentative or defensive in an unproductive manner.
CCSS.ELA-LITERACY. SL.11-12.1.C Propel conversations by posing and responding to questions that probe reasoning and evidence; ensure a hearing for a full range of positions on a topic or issue; clarify, verify, or challenge ideas and conclusions; and promote divergent and creative perspectives.	When challenged or questioned, provides evidence to support or further explain ideas.	Responds to questions with minimal evidence or explanation.	Responds to questions with no evidence or explanation.
CCSS.ELA-LITERACY. SL.11-12.4: Present information, findings, and supporting evidence, conveying a clear and distinct perspective, such that listeners can follow the line of reasoning, alternative or opposing perspectives are addressed, and the organization, development, substance, and style are appropriate to purpose, audience, and a range of formal and informal tasks.	Effectively and clearly presents information and supporting evidence in a creative, yet logical way that is precise and comprehensible. The audience is easily able to follow the speaker's line of thought. Highlights both strengths and limitations, connecting to learning style and habits outside the classroom.	Presents information, findings, and supporting evidence clearly and logically. The speaker's line of reasoning can be followed. Clearly explains strengths and limitations of skills, connecting to learning style and habits within the class.	Presents information and findings but lacks clarity and precision. Has supporting evidence but doesn't clearly make connections. Evidence is not concisely or logically presented. Only speaks to strengths or limitations.

FIGURE 46. "In defense of my work" handout. CCSS excerpted from CCSSI (2010).

7

Strategies for Reflecting to Learn

With the ILP model, you act as an experienced mentor who provides assistance through conferences, formative feedback, and low-stakes practice, moving students toward independence. Reflections are a primary method with which to monitor the pulse of each student as well as that of the class. Without reflection, we may not know the root of a student's frustration, or, worse yet, know that the student is frustrated at all. Many researchers hearken back to Dewey (1916) and this observation from *Democracy and Education: An Introduction to the Philosophy of Education*: "Thought or reflection . . . is the discernment of the relation between what we try to do and what happens in consequence. No experience having a meaning is possible without some element of thought" (p. 169). Without time and space for reflection, the learning process remains incomplete. In our rush to get through the curriculum, reflections sometimes fall by the wayside or become add-ons that are not integrated throughout the process of learning. To prevent this in our classrooms, we carve out multiple points in each unit for reflection *while* students are in the process of gathering information to respond to their questions and *while* they are simultaneously practicing skills. EQ reflections and standards reflections are placed after each round of activities in the ILP (see Figure 47). Though reflection does take time, that time is worth it, resulting in more efficient and effective learning in the end.

Each reflection is different. Even if an entire class is using the same EQ, or reading the same text, or studying the same standards, reflections are a chance for students to bring their own experience to those shared elements and articulate unique learning.

Strategy: Sharing the ISP Graphic

Students don't often think about their feelings while learning and how they might affect their abilities, but Kuhlthau (2004) did. Her ISP (see Figure 2) shows

Student Growth: The Learning Process and Reflections
Learning Activities: Throughout the course of the unit, you will complete nine activities. By the end of the ILP, you will be synthesizing what you've learned about your texts and research to help you better understand the essential questions, and all of the standards must be addressed at least once in each round.
Activity 1:
Activity 2:
Activity 3:
EQ Reflection 1: How do your texts and research help you answer your questions? What do you still need to learn?
Standards Reflection 1: What progress have you made toward your standards? What do you still need to learn?
Activity 4:
Activity 5:
Activity 6:
EQ Reflection 2: How do your texts and research help you answer your questions? What do you still need to learn?
Standards Reflection 2: What progress have you made toward your standards? What do you still need to learn?
Activity 7:
Activity 8:
Activity 9:
EQ Reflection 3: How do your texts and research help you answer your questions? What do you still need to learn?
Standards Reflection 3: What progress have you made toward your standards? What do you still need to learn?

FIGURE 47. "Student growth" from the ILP. Adapted from "The Role of Reflection in the Inquiry Plan," by M. Donhauser, H. Hersey, C. Stutzman, and M. Zane, 2015c, *School Library Monthly* (an imprint of ABC-CLIO), *31*(6), p. 8. CC BY-NC-SA.

students not only the thoughts and actions but also the feelings that occur at each stage of the process. It helps students to realize that this process occurs naturally—we just draw attention to it and sometimes slow it down through reflection and conferencing. We use it to explain why learning feels uncomfortable and messy sometimes. We make sure to explain that Kuhlthau (2004) did her research not just on students but also on research professionals, reiterating that getting comfortable with being uncomfortable is a skill they'll need throughout their lives. We often ask them to identify an emotion of the ISP that they are experiencing. At times, it is easiest for students to identify where they are in the learning process by determining how they are feeling at that moment. If they're in a negative place because they are unsure of what direction they are moving in, they are probably still in the *initiation* phase. However, if they are feeling negative because they are overwhelmed by information and possibilities, they are most likely in the *exploration* phase. Giving students these terms and sharing with them the natural stages they will experience helps us communicate better about where they are and how they are doing.

We also ask students to reflect on their learning habits. As Costa (2008) explained, "The intent is to help students get into the habit of behaving intelligently. A 'habit of mind' is a pattern of intellectual behaviors that leads to productive actions" (para. 6). Through us asking them to specifically think about their "patterns of intellectual behaviors," students begin to see where they can make adjustments to improve their productivity and their learning. To help them reflect on habits, we use a rubric designed from the language of the *Standards for the 21st Century Learner* (AASL, 2007) (see Figure 48).

Whether or not you use the ILP, this rubric can be used to summatively assess learning habits. As with any other reflection or self-assessment, we also ask students to determine steps toward future growth based on the criteria within the rubric. In the example shown in Figure 49, Peyton explains how repeatedly practicing skills helped her improve, and she also determines a plan for improving her participation and work habits.

Like Peyton, Jack (Figure 50) identifies an area of growth, pointing out, on the habits rubric, a specific aspect that he needs to improve. Since students will be able to apply these habits to many different scenarios, reflecting on learning habits is just as important as reflecting on reading or writing skills. It also allows them to celebrate their successes while realizing there is always room for improvement.

Habits Rubric			
Criteria	Advanced Proficient (A)	Proficient (C)	Developing (F)
Learning Process AASL: 1.4.3, 2.2.4, 4.1.8, 2.1.2, 2.4.3, 2.4.4, 4.1.6	Thoughtfully and creatively fulfills all assignments. Work shows a clear progression from one assignment to the next, demonstrates evidence of successful inquiry, and supports the final assessment.	Fulfills all assignments. Some aspects of completed work may not support inquiry or final assessment. Learning progression may be unclear.	Not all assignments completed. A strong disconnect between work, inquiry, and/or final assessment. Learning progression is unclear.
Work Ethic AASL: 1.1.9, 1.3.4	Student is actively engaged in learning, challenging oneself throughout the unit. Student is eager to develop knowledge and skills and share learning with teacher and classmates. Assignments are timely. Student takes responsibility for class materials and property.	Student is engaged in learning, occasionally sharing knowledge, insights, or resources with teacher and classmates. Student may need occasional reminders to stay focused on coursework. Assignments are timely, with perhaps a rare exception. Student occasionally lacks responsibility for class materials and property.	Student is detached from learning, often needing reminders to focus on coursework. Student may detract from others' learning. Assignments may be late or missing. Student routinely lacks responsibility for class materials and property.
Information Search Process and Inquiry AASL: 1.1.4, 1.2.2, 1.4.2, 1.4.4	Student uses feedback to develop understanding. Student is able to overcome obstacles such as time constraints and missteps in a professional manner. Student is curious and solves problems by using resources available. Student takes responsibility for the accuracy of sources and information.	Student uses some feedback to develop ideas, but may not respond to feedback that challenges thinking Student is reluctant to reach outside "comfort zone." Student relies on teacher for sources and information.	Student does not respond to feedback. Student is content to be lazy, setting easily achievable goals. This opportunity is totally lost on this individual. Student uses inaccurate information.

FIGURE 48. Habits rubric. CC BY-NC-SA. AASL standards excerpted from *Standards for the 21st Century Learner* (AASL, 2007, pp. 4, 5, 7).

> Two things that I have improved upon so far this year in English are writing and Socratic seminar. My writing has improved because we wrote lots of mini stories leading up to our final short story and I feel that doing these helped me prepare better. I feel that I have improved on my performance in Socratic Seminars by speaking up more, asking more questions, and giving insightful comments.
> Two things that I can improve on for the next unit is speaking up more in class and giving more input, I can do this by participating more and maybe asking more questions.
> Another thing I will do is to try to spend more time on vocab assignments each night. I will do this by setting time aside to complete some of it each day rather than doing it a few days before its due.

FIGURE 49. Peyton's goal setting.

> I could try to share more of my knowledge, insights, or resources with classmates or the teacher because I typically keep my thoughts to myself.

FIGURE 50. Jack's goal setting.

Strategy: Vocabulary for Reflecting

Before students can identify their own needs and assess their skills, they need to be given the tools to articulate their growth. As we mentioned previously, you can ask students to score themselves on a rubric or rank their performance. To further students' abilities to reflect on their learning, we should provide them with the vocabulary to do so. In Chapter 4, we discussed how close-reading and designing rubrics help students to understand the actions they are taking. Burke (2014) created "The A list" of academic vocabulary featuring words—*analyze, argue, compare/contrast, describe, determine, develop, evaluate, explain, imagine, integrate, interpret, organize, summarize, transform, support*—that allow students to more easily reflect on their performance of the standards.

In addition to Burke's list, we have found the actions and adjectives detailed in Figure 51 useful for our students as they reflect and self-assess. Meg uses these words to make up vocabulary lists for her various units, so that students can use them not only in their reflections and assessments but also in their various activities as well.

Actions	Adjectives
advance, articulate, collaborate, comprehend, converge/diverge, distinguish, embed, emerge, emulate, enhance, impute, infer, initiate, inquire, juxtapose, manipulate, reconcile, refine, scrutinize, substantiate, synthesize	coherent, complex, cumulative, exemplary, explicit, exposition, hackneyed, impetuous, inconsequential, mundane, objective/subjective, substantive, wary

FIGURE 51. Vocabulary of learning.

Strategy: Reflecting on EQs

EQ reflections first ask students to show their thinking about the content in writing. They synthesize the texts they've read and consider what those texts reveal about their questions. Reflections are not meant to be assessed for grammar or writing ability; they are truly a space where students should feel comfortable to let ideas flow, to discover what the texts and their experiences reveal. As one student, Juliet, affirmed:

I wrote my EQ reflection as I was thinking rather than planning first, and it led to writing down these great ideas I didn't even realize I had. I was informal, to the point, and brutally honest. Any thought I had I wrote, which lead to gems.

EQ reflections also require students to refine their questions because they need to ask themselves "What have I learned?" and "What do I still need to learn?" Since reflections encourage synthesis of texts, information, and personal insights, students will have experiences like Liz's:

My questions evolved a lot over the course of the unit because as I would find more information and answer certain questions, more questions always came up. I also learned throughout the course of the class that questions are endless and one question will always lead to another.

Alex, a sophomore honors student working through an ILP, demonstrated our four goals of a successful reflection:

1. identify current answers to questions
2. synthesize work to show the process of reaching a conclusion
3. give evidence of learning
4. refine questions and explain what still needs to be learned.

While studying the book *All Quiet on the Western Front*, he decided to examine how a person's inner conflicts are revealed during war. In just two rounds of activities, he made huge leaps in his understanding. Initially, he considered just one conflict: the individual's survival versus nationalistically driven conquest (see Figure 52). In a later reflection, after finishing the novel and exploring new sources, Alex realized that his original thinking was based on incomplete information (see Figure 53).

Alex's EQ reflections make his thinking visible. He critiques himself, and he explains how he is coming to his new understandings by exploring and synthesizing the texts from his second round of activities. By seeing not only what Alex thinks but also how he made his discoveries, his teacher or peers can jump in to ask questions that could extend that exploration even more. For example, following the EQ reflection in Figure 53, Cathy pushed Alex to go even deeper into the breakdown of personal identity that he saw in Paul during his homecoming

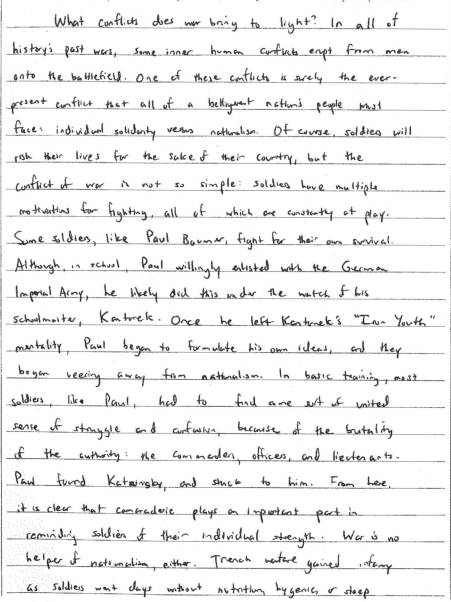

Essential Question Reflection: How do your texts and research relate to each other and to historical, modern, or personal examples? How does your work answer your questions?

What conflicts does war bring to light? In all of history's past wars, some inner human conflicts erupt from men onto the battlefield. One of these conflicts is surely the ever-present conflict that all of a belligerent nation's people must face: individual solidarity versus nationalism. Of course, soldiers will risk their lives for the sake of their country, but the conflict of war is not so simple: soldiers have multiple motivations for fighting, all of which are constantly at play. Some soldiers, like Paul Baumer, fight for their own survival. Although, in school, Paul willingly enlisted with the German Imperial Army, he likely did this under the watch of his schoolmaster, Kantorek. Once he left Kantorek's "Iron Youth" mentality, Paul began to formulate his own ideas, and they began veering away from nationalism. In basic training, most soldiers, like Paul, had to find some sort of united sense of struggle and confusion, because of the brutality of the authority: the commanders, officers, and lieutenants. Paul found Katzinsky, and stuck to him. From here, it is clear that comraderie plays an important part in reminding soldiers of their individual strength. War is no helper of nationalism, either. Trench warfare gained infamy as soldiers went days without nutrition, hygiene, or sleep

FIGURE 52. Excerpt of EQ Reflection 1 from Alex's ILP (to see the full reflection, please refer to the online appendix).

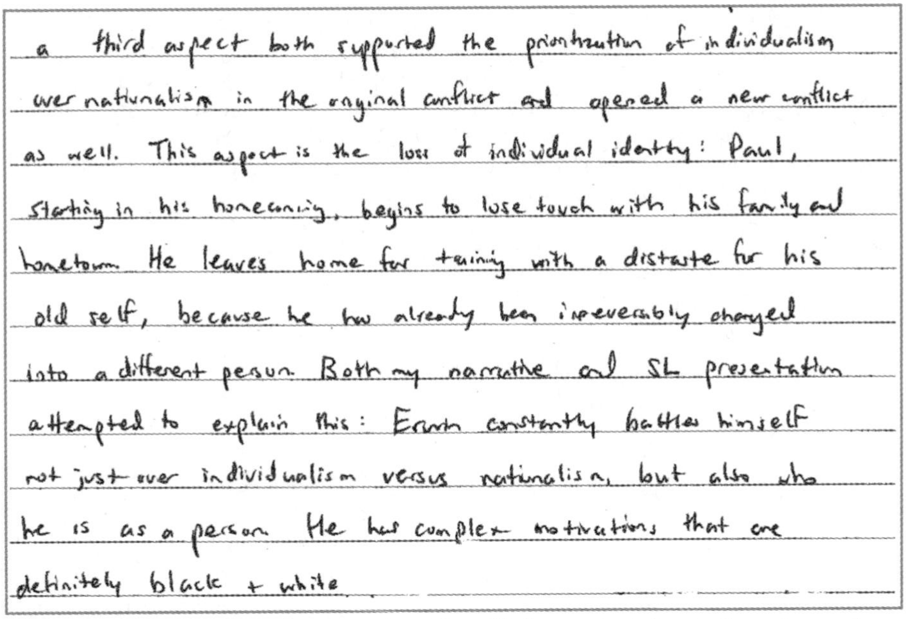

a third aspect both supported the prioritization of individualism over nationalism in the original conflict and opened a new conflict as well. This aspect is the loss of individual identity: Paul, starting in his homecoming, begins to lose touch with his family and hometown. He leaves home for training with a distaste for his old self, because he has already been irreversibly changed into a different person. Both my narrative and SL presentation attempted to explain this: Erich constantly battles himself not just over individualism versus nationalism, but also who he is as a person. He has complex motivations that are definitely black + white.

FIGURE 53. Excerpt of EQ Reflection 2 from Alex's ILP (to see the full reflection, please refer to the online appendix).

and asked him to consider some contemporary or personal examples of identity. More broadly, she asked Alex what new questions he had after he discovered that conflicts are not concrete, and then asked him why he thought humanity creates this dynamic.

For students who excel in speaking or who struggle with writing, spoken reflections can be very helpful, and we have each had students provide video reflections, in which they talk through their learning. One sophomore, Zach, recorded himself several times while reading his book, *The Devil in the White City*. He shared connections he was drawing, and he talked through the mysteries of the book. Eventually, this helped him to articulate a theme and to practice using evidence to support his ideas. And his teacher, Cathy, also got valuable insight into Zach's reading strategies. She could see when he couldn't wait to talk about something as well as when he struggled to reach understanding.

Pitfall: When Students Report Rather Than Synthesize

Synthesis is an essential skill for reflections, but often students end up just reporting what they've learned. Suzanne Vrancken, a special education in-class support teacher, helps students understand the process of synthesis with a graphic that demonstrates how to blend sources in response to their EQs (see Figure 54). She uses images to highlight the difference between synthesis and simply reporting on what each source indicates.

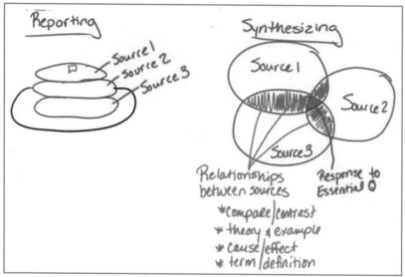

FIGURE 54. Pancaking. Reproduced with permission from Suzanne Vrancken. Reproduced from "The Role of Reflection in the Inquiry Plan," by M. Donhauser, H. Hersey, C. Stutzman, and M. Zane, 2015c, *School Library Monthly* (an imprint of ABC-CLIO), *31*(6), p. 9. CC BY-NC-SA.

As shown in Figure 54, Suzanne likens "reporting" to stacking pancakes. "Yes, there are similarities," she will explain, "and that's why they're all on the same plate together, but Pancake 1 has very little to do with Pancake 2." Hence, when students simply stack information about one source on top of information from another source, she refers to it as "pancaking." Using this technique, students only make very general statements, such as "War is an important theme in Realism." To remedy this, Suzanne explains *synthesis* and sets an important goal for her students: to blend sources by understanding how they relate. She refers to that "blend" as a conversation among the writers. She also suggests a few possibilities for making connections. For example, one source might illustrate a cause of an event and another might illustrate an effect; one might give a theory, and another exemplify proof for it. Once students are able to identify relationships, their next step is to synthesize the sources in writing to determine where they all meet to answer their EQs.

This is an especially important skill as it provides an opportunity for students to learn from their texts rather than find texts that merely reinforce what they already think, which is often the unwanted result of reporting or "pancaking." In order to synthesize, students have to first look at what the texts tell them, then put these strands in conversation to find a response to the EQ.

Strategy: Annotating Model EQ Reflections

Before a student's first attempt at an EQ reflection, it is a good idea to exemplify the expectations. Meg created an annotated model from an EQ reflection by Tyler, a former student (see Figure 55); her comments explain the steps the writer took in demonstrating his thinking.

For another, slightly more student-driven technique, students could also annotate a model reflection. In doing so, students look for evidence of the four goals of a successful EQ reflection:

1. current answers to questions
2. synthesis of resources
3. evidence of learning/thinking
4. question refinement

Students then emulate those requirements in their own reflections.

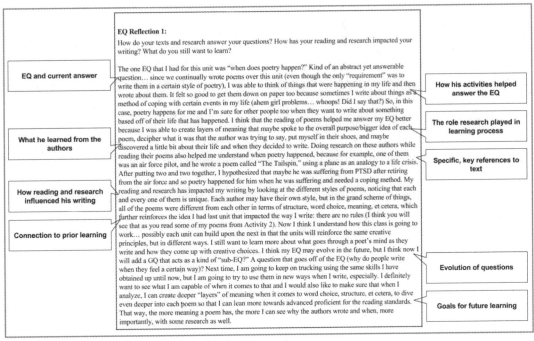

FIGURE 55. Annotated model of an EQ reflection (excerpt).

Strategy: Reflecting on Standards

Once students have assessed their work and identified their strengths and needs, it is important that they set goals for future activities. For most, it may be as simple as articulating how they plan to move from "Proficient" to "Advanced proficient." For others who have met the advanced proficiency requirements, they can think of how to combine multiple standards or incorporate more difficult texts. Once they have set their goal, they can identify it on the next activity, perhaps writing it at the top to keep themselves focused throughout the activity completion. Ideally, a standard reflection covers these four components:

1. identifies areas of strength
2. identifies areas for improvement
3. assesses each skill using the rubric criteria
4. sets goals for future activities

Excerpts from Alex's standards reflections (presented in Figures 56 and 57) follow his assessment and growth in his reading activities. For his first round, Alex identified and analyzed major themes in *All Quiet on the Western Front* to meet the standard:

CCSS.ELA-Literacy.RL.9-10.6: Analyze a particular point of view or cultural experience reflected in a work of literature from outside the United States, drawing on a wide reading of world literature. (CCSSI, 2010)

He used the rubric for the reading standard (as well as for each of the other standards in his first round of activities) to assess his work and set goals. Figure 56 is an excerpt from this reflection.

Alex is especially good at pointing out where he needs improvement, and it is clear that he plans to address those areas in the next round of activities. Because this activity is assessed formatively and not graded, he feels at liberty to provide an honest assessment of his work. However, he is much less specific when he discusses his strengths, using sentences like, "I really did well." While this is a positive sentiment, it doesn't reveal much about his particular skill abilities. This provides an opportunity to gather more information in peer review or in a teacher conference. For example, a reviewer could ask for evidence of something he described as "doing well" in his analysis.

Standard Reflection: What progress have you made towards your standards?

I chose R6, W3, SL3, and L5 as my standards for this unit. For R6, I attempted to outline book events in their historical context, but this didn't really satisfy the standard by neglecting P.O.V. in the book. I also didn't discuss figurative language very much. The only thing I really did well was interpreting events in historical contexts. I need to either revise the current activity a lot or create a new activity that would better satisfy the standard.

FIGURE 56. Excerpt of Standards Reflection 1 from Alex's ILP (to see the full reflection, please refer to the online appendix).

After practicing these activities again with new texts and new parts of the novel, Alex realized that he had hit a point of confusion. His next standard reflection (Figure 57) reveals a thoughtful and honest assessment of his reading skills and his understanding of the standard's requirements.

Standard Reflection: What progress have you made towards your standards?

This card, I realized that my first round of activities was pretty shabby, and did not satisfy any of the standards to my satisfaction. R6 needed me to describe an experience, but I'd only discussed one or two perspectives: authority and individuals. I did analyze the way those few perspectives impacted theme, but I didn't have enough perspectives. I still don't, and I need to fix that by Round 3. I also didn't try to distinguish the author's meaning from the speaker's pov because I still don't understand this requirement.

FIGURE 57. Excerpt of Standards Reflection 2 from Alex's ILP (to see the full reflection, please refer to the online appendix).

Because he has written, "I didn't try to distinguish the author's meaning from the speaker's [point of view] because I still don't understand this requirement," his teacher, Cathy, is able to identify a need to make sure that this is rectified before Alex makes his next attempt at that standard. Alex also reveals several specific goals for improvement, such as incorporating more perspectives to describe an experience in his reading activities. Articulating these important goals for learning is crucial throughout the process for students to move past the moments of uncertainty, confusion, frustration, and doubt that Kuhlthau's (2004) ISP (see Figure 2) recognizes as precursors to moments of clarity, confidence, and satisfaction.

"So What?"

8

We once needed teachers and textbooks to pass down dates, facts, and anecdotes, but we now have the internet to give us the details about any major event or figure. When we have all of this information at our disposal, education becomes less about "knowing" and more about "doing"—what are you going to *do* with all that you have learned? Richardson (2012) expanded on this idea in *Why School?*: "I'd rather know that my kids were creating something of meaning, value, and, I hope, beauty for people other than just their teachers, and that those creations had the opportunity to live in the world" ("Do Real Work for Real Audiences," para. 6). He wants all learners to move their learning outside the walls of school. When we let go of the control, the responsibility to answer the question "Why are we learning this?" returns to the students. After they have completed their learning activities and reflections, they have so much knowledge about a topic they are invested in, and they have developed skills that were lacking before. They've learned all this—so what?

To answer this question, we assign a "So what?" final assessment at the end of an ILP unit. Unlike the strategies we have discussed earlier in this book, we recommend treating the "So what?" element as a process rather than as independent strategies. Though it is adaptable in some aspects, which we discuss throughout this chapter, we recommend using the three steps described in Figure 58. For us, "So what?" is the most authentic assessment of the unit and allows students to create a product that reflects their individual learning. That's why it is our final stage of an ILP; however, it can also be used on its own as a final assessment for any unit.

Step 1: Synthesizing the Learning of the Unit

No matter how much control you've given your students during the unit, in the end, they develop an ultimate takeaway that is uniquely their own. Choosing the main lesson of the unit will be a very personal venture. Even if it's a unit in which students read the same text or ask the same EQ, their outcome will vary

So What?: The Outcomes
Now that you've developed your skills, learned new information, and gained insights, what are you going to do? This final project should be influenced by the work you've completed these past few weeks. • First, determine what the main lesson of this unit is. What is your takeaway in terms of the texts, standards, and essential questions? Then, decide who needs to know about what you've learned. Is there an important skill or lesson you want to share with others? Find an authentic audience and articulate why this person or group of people are the best audience for your lesson. What means will you use to communicate your discoveries? • Develop a rationale for your project in which you'll discuss how your work has inspired you. Using your texts and standards, explain what you'll do for your project in the space below. • Finally, create the product that you've outlined in your rationale and share it with your audience!

FIGURE 58. "So what?: The outcomes." Reproduced from "Final Product Assessment: So What?," by M. Donhauser, H. Hersey, C. Stutzman, and M. Zane, 2015d, *School Library Monthly* (an imprint of ABC-CLIO), *31*(7), p. 10. CC BY-NC-SA.

based on how their personal views shaped their learning. For some students, the takeaway might be their answer to a question, but others might feel that a skill they mastered was the most important outcome. As students take the time to look over their activities and reflections and to articulate the main lesson, you can conference with them to touch base about what they learned. Students should also take this time to meet in inquiry circles to discuss the unit; even if they did not read the same text, their peers have been a resource throughout the process and will be able to help point out the areas where they were excited about their learning. Even if you cannot complete the remaining steps of the "So what?" section, we encourage students to synthesize their learning and identify the main takeaway. It can serve as a concluding reflection for the unit; students also can share their major insights with one another during a final discussion.

One of the most common takeaways students will want to explore in their "So what?" is the answer to their EQ. Because the questions are often personally motivated, students are most connected to this section and want to share it with others. As a sophomore, Bria developed the EQ "Is feeling guilty a choice?" during the class unit on Shakespeare's *Macbeth*. She wrote in her rationale:

> Throughout my inquiry I have learned that people can choose whether or not they feel guilty and how to deal with said guilt. One first has to accept that they have done something wrong . . . that goes against their morals. Once you accept your guilt and that you can't change your actions you have to forgive yourself in order to move on with your life without guilt weighing on your conscience. Macbeth's guilt about killing Duncan turned into paranoia and he became a ravenous killer, taking out anyone that was a threat to his power.

In her explanation, Bria references the text to illustrate how she arrived at her understanding.

Step 2: Finding an Audience

Once students decide on the main lesson of the unit, they will decide who needs to learn about this concept. Choosing an audience allows students to create a more *authentic* product because they have to decide the best approach for sharing their takeaway with their specific audience. To do so, we ask students to consider the following questions:

- Who are the stakeholders involved in or impacted by your topic?
- Which people or groups have the power to change from what you know?
- Who will most benefit from knowing what you know?
- What have other people said about your topic, and where is that information? How is it presented and to whom?

When they have decided on an audience, they'll explain these choices in a rationale, which includes examples from the unit to demonstrate why their takeaway is important and why their chosen audience needs to hear this message.

For example, some students learn a skill that they wish they had learned earlier in their education, as it had such an impact on their later work. Seniors Analisa, Aida, and Michelle completed a group "So what?" and explained the following in their rationale:

> We decided to choose *duende* as a topic because we felt that it is an element of writing that should be better utilized in high school English classes. As we learned to love the concept of *duende*, we created our target as the underclassmen because they are not aware of this element and we believed that if we were taught the idea of *duende* in our younger high school years, it would've greatly benefited us. Learning about *duende* could help create the perfect college essay or write up in that creative writing class. We were inspired by our work because we want our readers to feel emotion when they read. . . . We feel that it is important for other writers to feel the same way. We want to feel the *duende* when we are reading other people's work so that we are intrigued by their work. Specifically, we were greatly inspired by our mimic poems that taught us to focus on the factors that created *duende* in our specific authors writing. After [completing] our mimic poems we learned styles and unique characteristics. . . . By mimicking and putting our own spin into our own poetry we learned the tactics of creating *duende*.

For these young women at the end of their high school experience, learning how to add emotional resonance to their writing was a skill they wished they had had before. As a result, they decided to teach a class of ninth graders how to make their writing more effective. When they created their Prezi, they identified three characteristics that a successful piece of writing must have: (1) passion, (2) personal connection, and (3) an aspect of performance. Using examples from their peers and asking questions of the ninth graders, Analisa, Aida, and Michelle explained how word choice, phrasing, and structure could affect the reader. As the final part of their lesson, they had students take "Friday" by Rebecca Black, a pop song they felt lacked artistic meaning, and revise it for more artistic appeal using the skills the girls had reviewed. This "So what?" addressed both the content (e.g., *duende*) and skills of the unit, so choosing an audience that could immediately put it into practice was a wise decision.

Pitfall: When They Can't Find an Audience

Finding an authentic audience is crucial to the success of the "So what?" section. Students often struggle with being shy and not wanting to share their work with anyone beyond the teacher; sometimes, even sharing with their classmates feels like a challenge. If you encourage students to share their work throughout the process, though, they will slowly become more comfortable with having others look at their thinking and products. We require that our students share with people outside of the classroom, but, even so, this might just be the school principal or school newspaper. However, we do encourage students to move outside the school in order to really drive home the fact that learning does not exist just within the confines of a school. Nevertheless, students sometimes just don't know where to look for audiences—their world is often their school, so they do not have many connections in the wider community. This is where your school librarian can step in to show students how to search online for local offices and public individuals that might find their work of value. It also helps to refer students back to the questions in Step 2, so that you can brainstorm ideas for finding a specific audience together.

Bria, the sophomore student who was studying guilt while reading *Macbeth*, decided to reach out to Casey Anthony, who, in 2008, was put on trial for the murder of her daughter. Bria explains why in the following rationale:

> [S]he has her freedom and in the eyes of the law she is innocent. Despite being able to freely do what she pleases, she is still trapped because of her guilt [Bria outlines why she believes this in a letter shown in "Step 3"]. She will always have to live with what happened to her daughter and that she didn't protect Caylee. . . . I have no intention of telling her how horrible of a person she is, I just want to explain to her that she isn't truly free until she forgives herself for having any part in her daughter's death because it is essential to her moving on with her life.

This authentic audience allowed Bria to research aspects of a controversial case and to apply her learning to it.

Another option is to assign an audience. We have done this previously with end of the course assignments whereby students write letters to future members of the class using the knowledge and skills they have gained in the course, so they remain very individualized. Even when an audience is assigned, there can still be choice. For example, students might be required to address an audience within their school, but they could decide which person to write to.

Step 3: Determining the Best Way to Reach Their Audience

When students first find out that they don't have to write a traditional essay for their "So what?," they are usually very excited! However, when they are then told the possibilities are completely open but they must be purposeful, they begin to grow a little apprehensive. Often, students will fall back on what they know—PowerPoint—and basically create an essay on slides, possibly with a few cartoons or animations thrown in. Done well, PowerPoint presentations can be an effective tool for a specific audience, but we try to push our students to look beyond the familiar, referring them to the multiple intelligences practice that we described in Chapter 5. As students think through potential mediums, they may want to consider the following questions:

- How does my audience receive information? What are some qualities of those mediums?
- What does my audience value?
- Will my audience need background information or certain terms defined?

In Cathy's honors sophomore course, one student was a talented musician and decided to compose a piece of piano music that depicted the struggle between Desdemona and Othello in *Othello*, using music composed on white keys to represent Desdemona and black keys for Othello. The harmony of his music matched the tone of the play, creating an auditory experience to enhance the text; it was a tool that future classes used when studying the text to gain a better understanding of the conflict. One of Meg's students, who was studying rape culture, created a YouTube video for teens using Robin Thicke's song "Blurred Lines"; the student's video contained images of rape victims sharing the words of their assailants, which were frighteningly similar to Thicke's lyrics. The student purposefully chose a popular song that would speak to teens and make an impact. This is why keeping the audience in mind is so important and

Pitfall: When They Don't Hear Back

Part of the excitement of having a real live audience with which to share one's learning is the anticipation of a response. When our students hear back from their audience, they feel proud (and sometimes terrified). Unfortunately, even when students put their hearts into their products, they sometimes don't receive responses from their intended audiences, especially when they have chosen an audience like the president or a celebrity. We don't want to set our students up to think that hearing back determines success, so we explain that there is no guarantee of a response, but they should create their products with the thought that their audience *will* be seeing it. This is another reason to think more locally about audience since they are more likely to receive a response from the mayor than the president.

why we have students choose their audience before their product. This way, they can step into their audience's place and determine the best way to reach them.

Bria, who had chosen Casey Anthony as her audience, wrote a letter that demonstrated her deep understanding of how guilt can affect a person and why it is so necessary for people to forgive themselves:

> I can't attest to your innocence because I wasn't there, but I can tell you that you are free by no means. It's not just because you have to live in a secret location unable to walk around a corner like an average person because of the extremely angry people that wouldn't think twice about harming you. It's because you are always going to feel guilty about what happened to your daughter no matter how small or large of a part you had in her death. She was still your child to protect and she died under your care. That fact will always weigh heavily on your conscience until you can find a way to let it go. I'm not saying you shouldn't care about what happened, but you need to forgive yourself and those around you so that you can move on and live a healthy life free of guilt trapping you inside yourself.

Bria successfully tied a very personal connection to a bigger audience, using one of the most intimate forms of communication, a letter. As a result, her product was a meaningful synthesis and reflection of the unit not only for her but for her audience as well.

Strategy: Replacing an Exam with a "So What?" Section

One major issue we have encountered is running out of time to complete the "So what?" element for every unit, especially when units needed to be lengthened because students struggled with the ILP process itself and required time to become more comfortable with this type of learning. When it isn't feasible to complete a "So what?" at the end of each unit, we still make sure to do one at least once. Sometimes, we combine units and ask students to do a "So what?" at the halfway point of a course. The experience of a "So what?" is an important one, so we've even had students create one in place of a course's final exam. Figure 59 shows how Meg adapted the "So what?" for a final exam project: students reflected on the entire course, which required them to think about content, skills, habits, and the learning community itself.

Honors Imaginative Process Final Exam

Each unit, you completed reflections that demonstrated what you learned about the literature and craft. For the exam, your focus will be shared with what you now know about the learning process and what you know about yourself as a learner. Because this is a course "So What?," you will need both a rationale and an artifact. Using the content and the learning experience of this course, determine what the main lesson of this course is. What is your take-away in terms of the texts, standards, and essential questions?

Then, decide who needs to know what you've learned. Is there an important skill or lesson you want to share with others? Find an authentic audience and articulate why this person or group of people is the best audience for your lesson. What means will you use to communicate your discoveries? Develop a rationale for your project in which you'll discuss how your work has inspired you. Using your texts and standards, explain what you'll do for your project in the space below.

Finally, create the product which you've outlined in your rationale and share it with your audience! Please refer to the "So What?" Rubric. This will be completed in small groups— at least 4, but no more than 7. I can place you in a group if you want. This means you will need to discuss as a group what the biggest take away is— you will also receive the same grade, unless something is really awry.

Your final product should be able to stand on its own; it should be an artifact of your learning. You will create this final product, not bring in an object that represents your main idea. Products might include videos, plays, board games, artwork, etc. The product should be able to be archived. Your rationale will explain the artifact and your sources for the final product will be your learning plans; while you may quote the literature and research, you will largely be citing your own work.

Some guiding questions:
- What have you learned about education, school, etc.?
- What have you learned about the process of learning?
- What have you learned about yourself? This must include being a student, but can also stem into other aspects of your life.
- How has your HIP experience been different from other learning experiences, whether in school or out?

Your ultimate "So What?" must fulfill the following standards adapted from the CCSS:
- Cite strong and thorough evidence to support analysis.

continued on next page

FIGURE 59. Sample use of "So what?" as an Honors Imaginative Process final exam.

FIGURE 59. Continued

- Determine two or more themes or central ideas of your inquiry and analyze their development over the course of the class, including how they interact and build on one another to produce a complex account.
- Develop the topic thoroughly by selecting the most significant and relevant facts, extended definitions, concrete details, quotations, or other information and examples appropriate to the audience's knowledge of the topic.
- Provide a concluding statement or section that follows from and supports the information or explanation presented (e.g., articulating implications or the significance of the topic).
- Present information, findings, and supporting evidence, conveying a clear and distinct perspective, such that listeners can follow the line of reasoning, alternative or opposing perspectives are addressed, and the organization, development, substance, and style are appropriate to purpose, audience, and a range of formal and informal tasks.
- Make strategic use of digital or physical media (e.g., textual, graphical, audio, visual, and interactive elements) in presentations to enhance understanding of findings, reasoning, and evidence and to add interest.
- Use prior and background knowledge as context for new learning.

Planning Help
- Review **all of your learning plans** to reflect on the progress you have made.
- What have been the outcomes of the course for you? What are the takeaways in terms of skills, content, and understandings? Things to consider as you reflect:
  - Information search process
  - Inquiry process
  - Habits of Mind
  - Your learning style
  - The literature you've studied

Some questions that might help:
- Have you applied any of those skills, content, or understandings to other areas of your life? If so, how? If not, how could you?
- What things did you find difficult or uncomfortable? How did you overcome these moments? Were they valuable to your learning? Why or why not?
- Which is more important— the process of learning or the product of learning? Why?
- In the beginning of the course, we familiarized ourselves with library resources and Google Docs. Which tools are most helpful? Least? Did you use any other web 2.0 tools? Did you use any of the web tools outside this class— either voluntarily or not? If so, how did you use them?
- How did you use your time in class and out of class? How much work did you do at home for this course? What kind of work did you do? What would have motivated you to work more diligently?
- What's the best classroom set-up (the physical space in the room, the arrangement of desks, etc.) for this course's structure?
- What limited you in this class, and what effect did that have on you or your learning?
- In what ways did you collaborate with your classmates? With your teachers? How can we create a stronger classroom community? Would that be beneficial?

Because students are fully independent in their choices of texts, standards, and questions for this course, the one common experience all students have had is the learning process itself. As a result, many students end up reflecting on this process, sharing the greatest lesson on learning they've obtained. For some, it is about questions or work ethic. In Meg's Honors Imaginative Process course, a group of students developed a video to be shared with next year's writing students to encourage them to work with one another. They wrote in their rationale that:

> All group work brings is noise, distractions, and unnecessary conversations that are almost always off topic. Most of these things combined certainly wouldn't bring a student success in the classroom. . . . At the start of this semester, it was no secret that student's [sic] struggled in the work ethic category. With becoming sidetracked daily and not focusing on the workload, students did not realize the importance of combining ideas. Over time, everyone began to notice that it was essential to keep up with all of our assignments. In order to complete these assignments, we found that working together increased the quality of our work. When everyone speaks their mind, it sparks new ideas that could lead any student to success. Feeding off of each other's points will allow the educated discussion to develop further. Our overall takeaway from this Honors Imaginative Process class was that unity, collaboration, and strong work ethic will benefit your overall experience in any class. . . . We all knew we would be pushed in this class due to the rigorous expectations, but for us four group members to be going on to college. . . . It was more than just about a letter grade in this class, it was about the learning styles and techniques that come along with struggling and adversity that we needed to overcome to help us define our learning foundation for the future.

Though these students read different texts and asked different questions throughout the course, they came together on the final exam to reflect on a unique experience they shared. This is valuable and can be done even if there aren't time constraints! If the sharing of the "So what?" needs to be adapted, students can use their classmates as their audience and complete a gallery walk or small-group presentation. This eliminates the need for the whole class to hear or see each one, and students still get to explain their greatest takeaway to multiple people.

Strategy: Assessing the "So What?" Section

When we assess the "So what?" section, we use a standards-based rubric that employs CCSS for English language arts and literacy (CCSSI, 2010), AASL (2007) standards from *Standards for the 21st Century Learner* (pp. 4, 6), and standards from the NCTE–International Reading Association's (1996) *Standards for the English Language Arts* (pp. 27–29) (see Figure 60; see also Chapter 3 for more information on standards). These standards are arranged by "ideas," "organization," "conventions," and "audience and purpose." Categories and standards allow you to assess the final product no matter what form it may take or what aspect of the plan was the student's greatest takeaway. The "So what?" section receives a summative grade, usually equivalent to an activity.

To create a successful *rationale* and *product*, the student should be inspired by the unit as a whole, and not just a single activity or text, and be able to explain how the knowledge and insight developed over time. Both the final product and rationale are assessed, since the rationale explains the work that led to the product, including synthesizing texts, skills, and/or dispositions.

How Long Does This Take?

The "So what?" element usually comes at the end of a unit that might last anywhere from three to ten weeks, depending on the curriculum and schedule. We devote at least three eighty-minute blocks to the "So what?," possibly more if it is done as a group or if it serves as a final exam. This allows students a block of time to formulate their ideas, a block to work on the rationale, and a block to execute the final product, in addition to spending some time working on it outside of school. For some students, the "So what?" may need to have more of a rolling deadline. For example, a group of seniors in one of Meg's classes decided to create bracelets to raise mental health awareness, which they had learned about over the course of the unit. These bracelets were designed quickly, but the students needed time to have their fundraiser approved by their administration. If you need to set a specific deadline, be sure your students know the dates up front and help them determine if their plan can be executed within the time frame given.

Though the "So what?" section can be tricky, it helps students to see the value behind their learning. When they share their final product with an authentic audience, whether it be a group of their peers, a local newspaper, or a leader in the community, it helps them see that their learning has value and that there is a reason that they're learning what they have. In his blog post discussing the importance of providing reasons for what students are learning, Lehmann (2013) explained, "When we challenge students to make connections between the content of the classrooms and the context of their lives, school can be more than preparation for real life. School can be real life" (para. 12). The ILP's "So what?" element blurs the lines between the classroom and the world outside it, allowing students to understand the impact they can have.

So What? Rubric			
Defining Traits	**Advanced Proficient**	**Proficient**	**Developing**
Ideas CCSS.ELA.CCRA.R.7 AASL 3.1.1 AASL 3.1.5 IRA/NCTE 8	Presents student's greatest takeaway from the unit and stems from synthesis of unit content/skills. Uses medium to provide insightful, original information while demonstrating deep knowledge of unit content/skills. Connects learning to community (local or global).	Presents student's greatest takeaway from the unit and stems from synthesis of content/ skills, but the connection may not be clear OR the synthesis lacks development. Uses medium to provide information that demonstrates comprehension of unit content/skills. Shows knowledge of community.	Presents student's takeaway, but its origins are not clear OR synthesis is weak or missing. Uses medium to provide information that demonstrates limited or incorrect comprehension of content/skills. Does not connect learning to community.
Organization AASL 3.1.4 CCSS.ELA.CCRA.W.4 OR CCSS.ELA.CCRA.SL.4	Builds an insightful product through effective organization and development. Clarifies relationships among ideas and reasoning with sophisticated and appropriate transitions. Enhances topic and purpose with meaningful structure.	Uneven organization and development restrict insight. Inconsistent transitions cause gaps among ideas and reasoning. Predictable or hackneyed structure.	Lack of organization and development prohibits insight. Lack of transitions leads to unclear relationships among ideas and reasoning Structure lacks meaning.
Conventions AASL 1.1.3	Presents an error-free product. Respects copyright/intellectual property rights of original creators and producers when using and creating media.	Some errors. Credits original creators but incorrectly or inconsistently.	Numerous errors take away from product. Does not credit original creators.
Audience and Purpose IRA/NCTE 7 AASL 3.1.3 CCSS.ELA.CCRA.SL.4 CCSS.ELA.CCRA.SL.5 OR CCSS.ELA.CCRA.W.4	Makes strategic use of the medium for an appropriate audience so that listeners or viewers can follow reasoning and purpose. Demonstrates awareness of audience's knowledge and interests. Communicates with audience in a timely and professional manner.	Appropriate medium but some disconnect within its delivery OR some of the audience's knowledge and interests are not addressed.	Disconnect between medium and audience OR unclear audience.

FIGURE 60. "So what?" rubric. Reproduced from "Final Product Assessment: So What?," by M. Donhauser, H. Hersey, C. Stutzman, and M. Zane, 2015d, *School Library Monthly* (an imprint of ABC-CLIO), *31*(7), p. 10. CC BY-NC-SA.

Pitfall: When a Product Doesn't Work

Even if the final product falls short, students can still do well in terms of a grade if the rationale explains the learning clearly and adheres to the criteria of the rubric; they may not receive an A, but they will not fail the assessment either. We encourage students to take risks throughout the process—to read challenging or obscure texts, to ask tough questions, and to design activities that take a different approach than just note-taking. This risk-taking tends to take center stage during the "So what?" process as students let their creativity reign. Sometimes though, the execution of these final products does not match what the creator intended. During one unit in an Honors Imaginative Process course, a student decided to write a poem to convey the motif of his unit (light and dark) and create a video of the poem being read to corresponding images. Poetry in itself is a complex skill; adding video creation to it can be a risk in terms of time management and creativity. Unfortunately, this student's risk did not pay off; while the poem was both technical and artful, the single image that repeatedly played in the background caused the product to fall flat. In situations like these, it's important to reward the risk and the work the student completed to support that risk. When assessed on the rubric, he scored low for "audience and purpose," particularly in the area of "disconnect with its delivery"; however, his rationale proved his intentions with the piece, so he scored well because his work "clarifies relationships among ideas and reasons," "enhances topic and purpose with meaningful structure," and "presents [his] greatest takeaway from the unit and stems from synthesis of unit content." Simply stated, taking risks doesn't preclude students from meeting requirements. This is a difficult lesson to learn, but a perfect one to learn as a teen. In fact, we encourage students to meet with us ahead of time. When they choose not to, they sometimes miss the mark. By not staking the entire grade on the actual product, students can be comforted knowing that the explanation of their thinking is as important as their creative skills, but they also know that blind risk will not be rewarded.

IV

Putting It All Together

Using the ILP so Students Can Take Control of Their Learning

Whew, we've done a lot of letting go so far, putting the responsibility for questions, texts, activities, and assessments into the hands of the students. Letting go requires trust in the process and a belief in the good that it does for students. To reiterate, we have discussed in prior chapters how letting go of each portion of unit design benefits student learning:

- Student choice of texts and questions increases buy-in, connects student interest to what they are studying at school, encourages a community of learners, and better prepares students for the future because they are able to find information that meets their needs and to create the questions to solve problems. (Chapters 1, 2, and 3)

- Working closely with standards and creating their own activities to build toward mastery of them enables students to peek behind the curtain of learning to see exactly what they are striving for and to create a plan for how to get there. (Chapters 4 and 5)

- Self-assessment and reflection provide students with a clear picture of their progress and insight into how they can transfer the knowledge and skills they have learned to new situations and contexts. (Chapters 6, 7, and 8)

Part IV focuses on a walk-through of the ILP, including assessment strategies. We also show you what using the ILP looks like in the classroom, from how teacher and student roles change to how you can use technology as a container for the plan. Last, Part IV details four different uses of the ILP so you can see how flexible and adaptable it can be.

9

ILP Walkabout

Giving students responsibility over any aspect of learning increases their knowledge of how they learn. When you turn over the whole kit and caboodle, the gains multiply. The ultimate in letting go is the ILP. This chapter explores key parts of the plan. Each foundational element is explained and exemplified with model student work. For a more thorough treatment of these foundational pieces, see the previous chapters, in which we break down strategies and explore pitfalls of each aspect:

- Chapter 1: Strategies for Beginning an Inquiry
- Chapter 2: Strategies for Choosing Texts
- Chapter 3: Strategies for Developing Questions
- Chapter 4: Strategies for Using Standards

This chapter also details the "Student growth" and the "So what?" sections of the ILP and provides two specific strategies for assessing the plan and its process. For further information on these aspects, see the previous chapters:

- Chapter 5: Strategies for Creating Activities
- Chapter 6: Strategies for Assessment, Feedback, and Conferencing
- Chapter 7: Strategies for Reflecting to Learn
- Chapter 8: "So What?"

So let's get started by reviewing the components of the ILP.

ILP

When students take responsibility for their own learning at this level, they will focus on three foundational elements: texts ("What I will read") as well as questions and standards ("What I will learn"). Everything goes back to and stems from at least one of those elements. Listing these elements at the top of the ILP serves as an overview for the activities, reflections, and final products that follow (see Figures 61, 62, and 63). Dana's sample ILP in this chapter represents one student's specific process, but, as explained in Chapter 1, there are many approaches to the ILP.

What I Will Read: Texts

Dana's example (see Figure 61) from a senior elective focused on narrative writing. Her list of texts shows a range of traditional literature from novels to microfiction and short stories. Dana also used additional nonfiction resources like Raymond Carver's essay "On Writing" to help her learn about the nuances of the craft, and news articles on sexual harassment to help her analyze the content of Joyce Carol Oates's *Foxfire*.

What I Will Read

In this unit, we will be exploring many texts together. You will also have the opportunity to choose some of your own. Be sure to keep this document updated!

1. Independent Read—*Foxfire* by Joyce Carol Oates
2. Microfiction—*Old Scars*
3. Microfiction—*With One Wheel Gone Wrong* by A.M. Homes
4. Microfiction—*The Wedding*
5. Independent Read—*And Then There Were None* by Agatha Christie
6. *The Woman Who Fooled Death Five Times: A Hwarhath Folk Tale* by Eleanor Arnason

During your exploration, you must also use additional resources to help you explore the time period, the authors, and/or the texts. These can be pieces of literary criticism, author bios, essays about the literary movements, etc. List those additional resources below.

1. "Why We Crave Horror Stories" by Stephen King
2. "The Uncanny" by Sigmund Freud
3. http://www.westernmassnews.com/story/24125055/pathfinder-high-school-accused-of-sexually-harassing-a-student
4. http://kfor.com/2014/04/03/oklahoma-teacher-charged-with-sexually-harassing-female-students/
5. "Feminism reflected in literature" by Eleanor B.
6. gender bias and feminist literature, From: *Encyclopedia of Feminist Literature*, Bloom's Literature
7. *On Writing* by Raymond Carver
8. Excerpts from *Bird by Bird* by Anne Lamott
9. http://www.dailywritingtips.com/8-steps-to-more-concise-writing
10. https://owl.english.purdue.edu/owl/resource/572/01/
11. http://www.readingrockets.org/strategies/descriptive_writing

---

FIGURE 61. "What I will read" from Dana's ILP.

While some units ask students to begin with core texts and then discover supplementary texts to assist them, sometimes students explore supplementary texts first. Dana's class began the unit by reading Stephen King's essay "Why We Crave Horror Movies" and Sigmund Freud's "The Uncanny." These two initial texts served as a springboard for her unit. Dana developed her questions, incorporating Carver's attention to writing style and Freud's use of fear and the unfamiliar. She then chose her core texts, including *Foxfire* and "The Woman Who Fooled Death Five Times: A Hwarhath Folk Tale," based on these concepts.

While texts can be the starting point, so can questions or skills as each plays a vital role in the overall development of the ILP. The starting point is simply the foundation that sparks initial interest in the inquiry. You can use any of the three (texts, questions, or skills) as the foundation for a unit depending on the goals and content of the course.

What I Will Learn: Questions

Questions, as described in Chapter 3, are used not only to understand texts but also to explore broader inquiries. Dana's questions in Figure 62 are broken down into EQs and GQs. Just as supplementary texts support core texts, GQs generally help students answer their EQs. Dana's EQs, broad and philosophical in nature, drove the scope of her unit, while her GQs, more specific in nature, were answered through careful analysis of texts and helped her gain crucial information for exploring the EQs she had developed. As you will see later in this chapter, Dana's questions evolved and multiplied as she gathered new information and analyzed new texts. Continually refreshing the list of GQs helped her gain more comprehensive answers to her EQs. While it may take only an activity or two to answer GQs, it's not until the end of the unit that she had a response to the EQs.

What I Will Learn: Standards

Standards capture the skills a student will practice over the course of the unit. They cover a range of skill types—reading, writing, language, and speaking/listening. Some students will also bring in standards from AASL, the International Society for Technology in Education, or NCTE, and some may even write their own for skills that are not captured anywhere else. In Figure 63, Dana lists nineteen standards from the CCSS. Each appears in Dana's activities at least three times over the course of her ILP. Nineteen standards seems like a lot, but it doesn't vary much from what teachers cover in a traditional unit. It's important

What I Will Learn

For this unit, you will be developing your own essential and guiding questions:

Essential questions
Why do humans like to be secretive about certain things?
Why do humans fear the unfamiliar, including death?·
Do any of us escape the things we fear?

Guiding questions
Can we find the uncanny within ourselves?
How can you create a sense of uncanny in your writing?
Can fear exist without the uncanny?
What do you consider uncanny?
What is achieved by using the uncanny in your writing?
Do we all experience uncanniness?
Are you always aware of your Other? Do you and your double always feel connected?
Is it a necessity for the double to represent darkness? Why or why not?
Do we all have an Other in our lives?
Why do most of us feel uncomfortable with our double that we choose a side and deny our Other?
Could a lack of knowledge be considered death? No growth...is that considered death?
How can someone with so little, feel like they have so much?

FIGURE 62. "What I will learn—Questions" from Dana's ILP.

to remember that Dana didn't complete an activity for each standard; rather, she combined many standards together. For example, Dana did not do a specific activity on punctuation, but instead practiced this skill throughout her writing activities.

Student Growth: The Learning Process and Reflections

Every ILP consists of three rounds of activities. Each activity is a work of synthesis, blending standards, texts, and questions. Students practice each of their standards in every round. Figure 64 illustrates each piece of Dana's "Student growth" section, so you can see an overview of her work. We have added highlights and comments to draw attention to what she was working on and what she accomplished (see also Figures 65–75, which are cited in this annotated table and featured in the following pages). The bolded pieces are discussed in detail in this chapter and include three of Dana's reading activities, one from each round, separated by EQ reflections and standards reflections. To see her completed ILP, please refer to the online appendix.

What I Will Learn

Reading Standards

2. Determine two or more themes or central ideas of a text and analyze their development over the course of the text, including how they interact and build on one another to produce a complex account; provide an objective summary of the text.

3. Analyze the impact of the author's choices regarding how to develop and relate elements of a story or drama (e.g., where a story is set, how the action is ordered, how the characters are introduced and developed).

Writing Standards

3. Write narratives to develop real or imagined experiences or events using effective technique, well-chosen details, and well-structured event sequences.

    a. Engage and orient the reader by setting out a problem, situation, or observation and its significance, establishing one or multiple point(s) of view, and introducing a narrator and/or characters; create a smooth progression of experiences or events.

    b. Use narrative techniques, such as dialogue, pacing, description, reflection, and multiple plot lines, to develop experiences, events, and/or characters.

    c. Use a variety of techniques to sequence events so that they build on one another to create a coherent whole and build toward a particular tone and outcome (e.g., a sense of mystery, suspense, growth, or resolution).

    d. Use precise words and phrases, telling details, and sensory language to convey a vivid picture of the experiences, events, setting, and/or characters.

    e. Provide a conclusion that follows from and reflects on what is experienced, observed, or resolved over the course of the narrative.

4. Produce clear and coherent writing in which the development, organization, and style are appropriate to task, purpose, and audience. (Grade-specific expectations for writing types are defined in standards 1–3 above.)

5. Develop and strengthen writing as needed by planning, revising, editing, rewriting, or trying a new approach, focusing on addressing what is most significant for a specific purpose and audience.

7. Conduct short as well as more sustained research projects to answer a question (including a self-generated question) or solve a problem; narrow or broaden the inquiry when appropriate; synthesize multiple sources on the subject, demonstrating understanding of the subject under investigation.

Language Standards

1. Demonstrate command of the conventions of standard English grammar and usage when writing.

2. Demonstrate command of the conventions of standard English capitalization, punctuation, and spelling when writing.

3. Apply knowledge of language to understand how language functions in different contexts, to make effective choices for meaning or style, and to comprehend more fully when reading or listening.

    a. Vary syntax for effect, consulting references (e.g., Tufte's *Artful Sentences*) for guidance as needed; apply an understanding of syntax to the study of complex texts when reading.

Speaking/Listening Standards

1. Initiate and participate effectively in a range of collaborative discussions (one-on-one, in groups, and teacher-led) with diverse partners on grades 11–12 topics, texts, and issues, building on others' ideas and expressing their own clearly and persuasively.

    a. Come to discussions prepared, having read and researched material under study; explicitly draw on that preparation by referring to evidence from texts and other research on the topic or issue to stimulate a thoughtful, well-reasoned exchange of ideas.

    b. Respond thoughtfully to diverse perspectives; synthesize comments, claims, and evidence made on all sides of an issue; resolve contradictions when possible; and determine what additional information or research is required to deepen the investigation or complete the task.

2. Integrate multiple sources of information presented in diverse formats and media (e.g., visually, quantitatively, orally) in order to make informed decisions and solve problems, evaluating the credibility and accuracy of each source and noting any discrepancies among the data.

FIGURE 63. "What I will learn—Standards" from Dana's ILP. CCSS excerpted from CCSSI (2010).

Element of ILP	Activity Descriptions
Activity 1 (Figures 9.5 & 9.6)	Reading instructions and activity: Analyzing theme and author's choices in book
Activity 2	Writing activity: Researching, analyzing, and writing first microfiction
Activity 3	Speaking/listening and writing activity: Research and small group discussion on the concept of "the Other" to inspire pre-writing for short story
EQ Reflection 1 (Figure 9.7)	
Standards Reflection 1 (Figure 9.8)	
Activity 4	Speaking/listening and writing activity: Research and present Feminism/Gender/Queer critical lens Write a microfiction twice: once with her own lens and once with a lens that another group researched
Activity 5 (Figure 9.9)	Reading activity: Analyzing theme and author's choices in a short story that relates to EQ
Activity 6	Writing activity: Research writing skills that are lacking and write a rough draft of a short story
EQ Reflection 2 (Figure 9.10)	
Standards Reflection 2 (Figure 9.11)	
Activity 7 (Figure 9.12)	Reading activity: Analyzing theme and author's choice in short story
Activity 8	Speaking activity: "In defense of my work"
Activity 9	Writing activity: Final draft of microfiction and short story, with evidence of revision
EQ Reflection 3 (Figure 9.13)	
Standards Reflection 3 (Figure 9.14)	
So What? (Figure 9.15)	

FIGURE 64. Overview of Dana's ILP (including descriptions of sections that are not featured in this book).

In Round 1, Dana made her first attempt at her reading standards by analyzing theme development in *Foxfire* as well as examining how the author's choices impact the theme. The excerpt in Figure 65 contains the instructions, using the language for standards CCSS.ELA-Literacy.RL.11-12.2 and CCSS.ELA-Literacy.RL.11-12.3 (CCSSI, 2010), that she wrote for her activity based on a class-created rubric. Grounding her work with this language sets her up for success in demonstrating the requirements of the standards. Dana took the standards and developed specific actions she could take to demonstrate mastery. She broke down her tasks into sections such as "take notes on key points of themes," "provide a short summary," and "bring in other works."

Instructions: Identify more than two sophisticated themes that go beyond a first read impression. In a paragraph, explain and track how the themes relate to each other and change throughout the story to impact the main idea of the text. Take notes on the key points of themes and analyze them. Provide a short summary that contains key points that help support the theme selection. Incorporate essential and guiding questions into the theme.

Analyze the author's choices for plot, structure, character, setting, tone, and more and how they relate to the theme. Take notes describing these choices. Bring in other works that have similar themes to aid to the discussion. Make sure your evidence is also relating to your essential and guiding questions. Sophisticatedly analyze the author's choices beyond the key elements.

FIGURE 65. Instructions for Activity 1 from Dana's ILP.

The excerpt shown in Figure 66 shows Dana's first attempt at meeting the requirements of the standards by following the instructions she set up (Figure 65). In this activity, Dana broke down *Foxfire*'s themes and examined the author's use of plot, structure, character, and tone to develop those themes. After identifying the author's choices, she connected them to the mistreatment and stereotyping of girls. This was a great first step because she began to touch on the skills necessary to show mastery in her reading standards and gained key insights that helped her answer her EQs. Activities 2 and 3 addressed her writing, language, and speaking standards (to see all three of Dana's activities from Round 1, please refer to the online appendix). After completing all three, she reflected.

Reflections are as crucial as the activities themselves. As explained in Chapter 7, EQ reflections have four main purposes:

1. to identify current answers to questions
2. to synthesize work and show the process of reaching a conclusion
3. to give evidence of learning
4. to refine questions and explain what still needs to be learned

Learning Activities: Throughout the course of each unit, you will complete nine activities. Remember, you are synthesizing what you've learned about your texts and research to help you better understand your essential questions, and all of the standards must be addressed at least once in the activities.

Activity 1:
Evidence is being used from the first 150 pages of *Foxfire*.

Themes:
❏ Gang life- life you would not otherwise experience; brutality; not asking for permission; bond of sisterhood; everlasting connections
❏ Feminism- strong, teenage girls; tough; ready for anything; don't look back; "Men are the enemy;" need for equality; women are as strong as men; sheds light up inappropriate ways men act and how it is not okay
❏ Bonds- *Foxfire* is linked together; shows true women and not predictable stereotypes

Paragraph:
I believe the whole purpose of this novel is to shed light on the need for equality between men and women. A girl gang is out to prove themselves as strong women who should not be treated any less respectfully just because of their gender. By working together to prove a point, the girls build a strong bond, and lessons about loyalty are taught.

The novel starts off by describing a gang life- from initiation to what acts they will be partaking in. Then, the novel begins to reveal that these girls are out to prove a point- men are not superior. Through the events of vengeance, the girls' great bonds can be displayed. All of these themes are connected.

Essential and Guiding Questions:
Uncanny-
❏ Not expecting girls to rise above men
❏ Different view of the world
❏ Makes us question what is real and what is not
❏ The society in the story is not real

Plot Structure
❏ Five girls try to attack a man who has made sexual advances on one of their friends; they are punished
❏ Girls work together
❏ Bonds are built when they are all accused
❏ Chronological
❏ Telling us what she remembers
❏ Shows how strong bonds are; she still remembers these people
Characters-
❏ Five girls and males who mistreat women
❏ Girls go against stereotypes
❏ Males are used to mistreat women; shows the reader how bad men are
Setting-
❏ A school
❏ Shows how bad men are that they even mistreat women in schools
❏ Male teachers are bad
Tone-
❏ Serious
❏ Mistreating women is taken very seriously
Other choices-
❏ Makes girls powerful
❏ Girls don't fall into usual stereotypes
❏ All of the males in the book are bad
❏ Girls get in trouble, even though boys should have
❏ All males mistreat women

All of these relate to the theme because the author makes specific choices in order to prove that girls should not be mistreated. The girls in the book are not stereotypes and all of the males in this book are at fault.

FIGURE 66. Round 1: Reading activity from Dana's ILP.

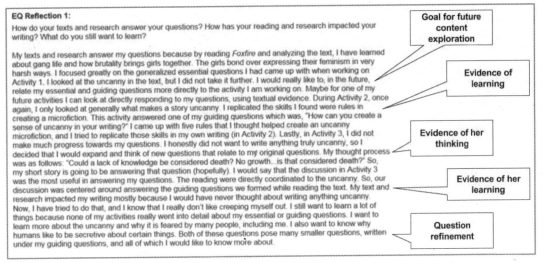

EQ Reflection 1:

How do your texts and research answer your questions? How has your reading and research impacted your writing? What do you still want to learn?

My texts and research answer my questions because by reading *Foxfire* and analyzing the text, I have learned about gang life and how brutality brings girls together. The girls bond over expressing their feminism in very harsh ways. I focused greatly on the generalized essential questions I had came up with when working on Activity 1. I looked at the uncanny in the text, but I did not take it further. I would really like to; in the future, relate my essential and guiding questions more directly to the activity I am working on. Maybe for one of my future activities I can look at directly responding to my questions, using textual evidence. During Activity 2, once again, I only looked at generally what makes a story uncanny. I replicated the skills I found were rules in creating a microfiction. This activity answered one of my guiding questions which was, "How can you create a sense of uncanny in your writing?" I came up with five rules that I thought helped create an uncanny microfiction; and I tried to replicate those skills in my own writing (in Activity 2). Lastly, in Activity 3, I did not make much progress towards my questions. I honestly did not want to write anything truly uncanny, so I decided that I would expand and think of new questions that relate to my original questions. My thought process was as follows: "Could a lack of knowledge be considered death? No growth...is that considered death?" So, my short story is going to be answering that question (hopefully). I would say that the discussion in Activity 3 was the most useful in answering my questions. The reading were directly coordinated to the uncanny. So, our discussion was centered around answering the guiding questions we formed while reading the text. My text and research impacted my writing mostly because I would have never thought about writing anything uncanny. Now, I have tried to do that, and I know that I really don't like creeping myself out. I still want to learn a lot of things because none of my activities really went into detail about my essential or guiding questions. I want to learn more about the uncanny and why it is feared by many people, including me. I also want to know why humans like to be secretive about certain things. Both of these questions pose many smaller questions, written under my guiding questions, and all of which I would like to know more about.

Goal for future content exploration

Evidence of learning

Evidence of her thinking

Evidence of her learning

Question refinement

FIGURE 67. EQ Reflection 1 from Dana's ILP.

In Figure 67, Dana's EQ reflection delivers on two of these purposes. Since Dana's course focused more on writing instruction, her EQ reflection connects her learning to her writing, rather than making historical or personal connections as is usually required. While Dana did provide an answer to her question from this round of activities, such as her rules for uncanny microfiction, she didn't demonstrate the synthesis required to reach those conclusions. In future EQ reflections, she should explain what information from each of her texts helped her to develop her rules. For example, were these traits in all of the works, and, if so, where?

Dana also showed her first attempts at self-assessment in her standards reflection (see Figure 68), in which she hit four key elements of this type of assessment:

1. identifying areas of strength
2. identifying areas for improvement
3. assessing each skill
4. setting goals for future activities

In addition, Dana noted her work in the scheme of Kuhlthau's (2004) ISP.

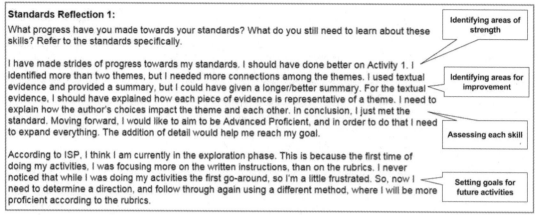

FIGURE 68. Standards Reflection 1 from Dana's ILP.

In Dana's second round of activities, she worked toward the goals she set in her reflections. To guide her learning, she listed the reading standards CCSS. ELA-Literacy.RL.11-12.2 and CCSS.ELA-Literacy.RL.11-12.3 (CCSSI, 2010) and the advice from her teacher to incorporate one of the critical lenses that the class studied (see Figure 69; the comments in the margin of the activity pinpoint her progress).

In her second round of activities, Dana had set out to learn about the following:

- "the uncanny and why it is feared by many people, including me"
- "why humans like to be secretive about certain things"

Figure 70 represents Dana's thinking after completing her second round of activities. She discusses whether she met the two learning goals listed above. This reflection is more sophisticated than her first in that she brought together all of her resources to show how they impacted her thinking. Synthesizing her texts with the work in her activities helped her reach her conclusion. She also recognized where she still needed to grow.

Dana showed similar strides in her assessment of her work with the standards. Within her standards reflection (see Figure 71), she indicates areas of strength and also pinpoints areas for improvement, which she uses to establish goals for her last round of activities.

1. Incorporate <u>one of the critical theories</u> into your examination of the themes of the story (so, how might a Marxist reading of the story impact the theme? How would that differ from a feminist reading?)

2. Determine two or more themes or central ideas of a text and analyze their development over the course of the text, including how they interact and build on one another to produce a complex account; provide an objective summary of the text.

3. Analyze the impact of the author's choices regarding how to develop and relate elements of a story or drama (e.g., where a story is set, how the action is ordered, how the characters are introduced and developed).

★ *The Woman Who Fooled Death Five Times: A Hwarhath Folk Tale* by Eleanor Arnason
  ○ Read
  ○ Annotated

★ Sociological/Marxist Archetypes
  ○ Superstition of death tells about the time period
    ■ Must be a long time ago, because now people are aware of what causes death. People no longer think about death coming in the ways they did in mythical stories.
  ○ Demonstrates education levels are low
    ■ People do not know much about death because they aren't well-educated . They make up stories about how people die, that we now know are not true, just made up myths. They used these myths in order to have an answer for things they did not know about. This further proves that they did not know the true causes of death.
  ○ People tell stories about death
    ■ People told stories about death in order to fill up the gaps of the unknown.
  ○ Death is unknown, so people create stories about it to feel a sense of comfort
    ■ Making up these stories provided comfort to the people who existed. The stories made people feel like they knew how death would come to them.
  ○ Impacts theme- creation; makes you think about creations/stories of the time period   ⟵ **Meeting the goal to connect analysis to elements of theme**
    ■ People of the time period lacked so much knowledge that they needed to make up stories about creation. They weren't as scientifically advanced, and therefore didn't know how babies were made.
  ○ Feminist reading=different- men oppress women...the man in the story is Death, and the woman is being oppressed by him
    ■ If I had read this through a feminist lens, I would have been very concerned about the fact that women were incorrectly portrayed in the story. They were under the mercy of a man; their death was in the hands of a man. I would not have liked this because their deaths should have been equally in the hands of a girl or a boy.

★ Themes:
  ○ The creator is a female because only woman can be impregnated.
  ○ There is a constant struggle between life and death.
  ○ Humans always have to suffer the consequences of bad actions.

★ Analyze Development Over Course of Text:
  ○ Quotes-   ⟵ **Meeting the goal to find quotes that directly develop the theme**
    ■ "The Goddess built the world."
    ■ "Because Death had not found her, she was not entirely dead. Rather, she existed in a strange place between life and death."
    ■ "Usually, people die the moment I pop them in my bag….The bad parts remain here as angry ghosts, complaining about their lives and deaths. Gradually, their anger wears them out. They grow thin and vanish entirely."
    ■ "But you are something new, neither alive nor dead."
  ○ Interact and Build-   ⟵ **Working toward the goal to demonstrate how each piece of evidence represents the theme**
    ■ Throughout the story, Ala , the main character, is trying to fool death. Death is male and the Goddess created Death. There is a reason the Goddess created Death and not the God: only girls can get pregnant and create beings. Furthermore, the male shows Ala she is struggling between life and death. The male is superior and in charge of the paths she follows in her life. She is constantly fighting Death, in order to not end her life. She deceives him greatly, but she is constantly struggling to stay alive. In the end, she faces consequences when she is stuck between life and death. It is not a desirable way to live. All in all, everyone has to battle between life and death, and everyone faces the consequences of their bad actions.

★ Summary of Text: ⟵ **Meeting the goal to provide a longer, more detailed summary**
  ○ A Goddess creates a character Death by pooping. He then knocks at Ala's door, and Ala pretends to be her sister when she answers. He does this five times, and each time, Ala tricks Death into taking something else home to kill. He never ends up killing Ala herself. Ala never dies, but she does not feel alive either. Ala goes to visit Death, and he tells her she is stuck between life and death.

FIGURE 69. Round 2: Reading activity from Dana's ILP.

continued on next page

FIGURE 69. Continued

★ Analyze:
  ○ Something is wrong, because Ala lives by herself. At the time, women weren't supposed to do that.
  ○ There was no clear ending.
  ○ The Goddess is stubborn. She doesn't die in the end, so did she really learn from her experiences?? (My thoughts)
  ○ After looking deeply into this...
    ■ Some people do not learn from experience.
    ■ Ala does suffer consequences to a certain extent-
      • She is trapped in Death's house
      • She is stuck in between life and death

★ Impact of Author's Choices:
  ○ Where is story set?
    ■ The story is set in Ala and Death's home.
      • This creates a sense of easiness with death. The reader should not be afraid of Death when we are reading about its home.
  ○ How is action ordered?
    ■ The action is ordered for the reader to eventually see the consequences of trying to evade death.
      • This creates suspicion of what happens when you are struggling between life and death. ◄———— Working toward the goal of explaining how the author's choices impact the theme
  ○ How are characters introduced and developed?
    ■ Death is introduced in the first line. He is developed through dialogue and actions, further proving the author's intentions to make Death personable.
  ○ Personification of Death-
    ■ The author personifies death in order to make death seem more relatable. Death in this story is more personable because he is human. He isn't a much greater being. Death talks, walks, makes facial expressions, and has feelings. Death's name is also capitalized in order to further prove its humanity. ◄———— Working toward the goal of explaining how the author's choices impact each other

★ Other Works:
  ○ http://listverse.com/2013/10/22/10-of-the-most-gruesome-deaths-in-mythology/
    ■ On this website, I read many myths about deaths. It was very interesting to find that in all of these myths, there is always a consequence to be faced, and always a struggle to face. Similarly, in this short story, Ala had to face the struggle of existing in a phase between life and death. She always exists like this because she is facing the consequences of going up against Death.

This is interesting because it probably wasn't even on their radar, right? They may have thought they were wise even if not educated.
Excellent
Oh yeah that's interesting--I wonder if there are death goddesses in some cultures and why in western civilizations we view death as male.
You could keep going with this and try to look at why there is always a struggle.
This is a main character or the goddess?
What kind of things? I wonder if they are symbolic at all.
Is she supposed to learn? This is what I'm thinking about now--is Death stronger than the goddess? And if so, what does that say?
Is this like purgatory?
So something about death being natural?
You could use more textual support here--what specific dialogue and what does it reveal?
And for some doesn't it prolong death? Like Sisyphys--he's tortured over and over but doesn't die.

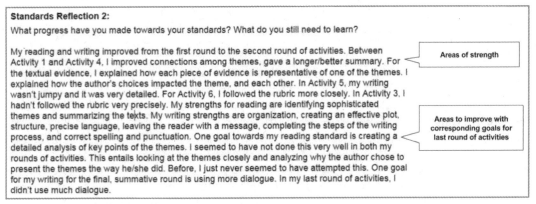

EQ Reflection 2:

How do your texts and research answer your questions? How has this work impacted your writing? What do you still want to learn?

The essential question I have been most directly answering is: "Why do humans fear the unfamiliar?" As of right now, I believe that people fear the unfamiliar because they do not know what it holds. People tend to dislike what they don't know because they are not comfortable with the idea of something out of their knowledge-range existing. For example, my brother asked me a couple of weeks ago, "Do you like alligator meat?" I immediately answered him, telling him I didn't. However, I have never tried alligator meat. Through Activity 4, I learned that perspective greatly impacts feelings. When I wrote my story through a feminist lens, I was more weary of gender equality. However, before I wrote my story from the perspective of a feminist, I was scared of thinking and writing like a feminist. I was fearful of the unknown. In the book *And Then There Were None*, each character fears how they will die. Interestingly enough though, they are more concerned with the unknown ways they may die in. This further proves my answer that people are afraid of the unknown because it causes them to think too much. We like what we know. In Activity 5, I read a myth about Death, called *The Woman Who Fooled Death Five Times*. This story helped me answer my EQ because I found that these people created stories about death because they feared the unknown. By creating stories about something that was out of their range of knowledge, they comforted themselves. Throught Activity 6, I learned that people don't like to accept what they don't know. I researched about the unknown, and I found out that people who travel the world and gain the most knowledge they can will be more successful in life because they went out of their comfort zones. This is what I portrayed in my short story; the less educated students didn't want to grasp the material because it was foreign to them. This round of activities, these were the GQs I've answered: "Could a lack of knowledge be considered death? No growth...is that considered death? and How can someone with so little, feel like they have so much?" The new GQ I have that I want to answer in the final round is, "Why do most of us feel uncomfortable with our double that we choose a side and deny our Other?" This is because I focused more on death and lack of knowledge this round, I'd really like to go back and focus on the Other again.

Callout labels: Overall learning, which stems from synthesis of her activities and resources; Evidence of learning; Evidence of learning; Evidence of learning; Question refinement

FIGURE 70. EQ Reflection 2 from Dana's ILP.

Standards Reflection 2:

What progress have you made towards your standards? What do you still need to learn?

My reading and writing improved from the first round to the second round of activities. Between Activity 1 and Activity 4, I improved connections among themes, gave a longer/better summary. For the textual evidence, I explained how each piece of evidence is representative of one of the themes. I explained how the author's choices impacted the theme, and each other. In Activity 5, my writing wasn't jumpy and it was very detailed. For Activity 6, I followed the rubric more closely. In Activity 3, I hadn't followed the rubric very precisely. My strengths for reading are identifying sophisticated themes and summarizing the texts. My writing strengths are organization, creating an effective plot, structure, precise language, leaving the reader with a message, completing the steps of the writing process, and correct spelling and punctuation. One goal towards my reading standard is creating a detailed analysis of key points of the themes. I seemed to have not done this very well in both my rounds of activities. This entails looking at the themes closely and analyzing why the author chose to present the themes the way he/she did. Before, I just never seemed to have attempted this. One goal for my writing for the final, summative round is using more dialogue. In my last round of activities, I didn't use much dialogue.

Callout labels: Areas of strength; Areas to improve with corresponding goals for last round of activities

FIGURE 71. Standards Reflection 2 from Dana's ILP.

In Activity 7 (see Figure 72), Dana's final attempt at the reading standards, she worked to analyze "why the author chose to present the themes the way he/she did." After completing two rounds of practice, reflecting, and receiving feedback, she was ready to showcase what she learned, which is why this activity was included in her final grade. All three activities in this final round of the ILP were scored summatively to capture abilities in each of the standard areas. This activity also captured her summary of the passage and listed the techniques that the author used to develop the theme. Additionally, Dana wrote an instrumental song with an explanation to illustrate her understanding of the author's craft (see the online appendix).

Activity #7

The Bank Robbery
By: Steven Schutzman

THEMES:

After a first read, there is an obvious theme at the core of this story: in the most unlikely situations, people can be brought together. The bank robber and the teller who he threatened, end up falling in love. Evidence of this can be found through the second-to-last sentence: "The bank robber and the bank teller left together like hostages of each other." So, in the most unusual situation, the robber and the victim fell in love. However, there are more complex themes that go beyond a first read of this story. *The Bank Robbery* contains a lot of symbolism of love that all connect to prove that love comes in all different shapes and sizes. The victim of the robbery says that danger is just like love. This means that love isn't always good for you; love can be dangerous. Furthermore, the robber equivalates money to love at the beginning of this story. This is saying that love can be bought. On one of the notes the robber writes the teller he says, "WHEN YOU RUN OUT OF MONEY YOU SUFFER." This is symbolic of the fact that when you run out of time, you die. I also think that the gun in this story is symbolic. In the notes that the robber writes the teller, the gun is used as a threat. The last sentence of the story is as follows: "He kept the gun on her, for it was becoming like a child between them." This is symbolic of the fact that danger can lead to love. Once again, love isn't always a good thing; in this case, the lovers created a gun (which generally has a negative connotation because it is used to kill people) as their child. The gun brought them together even though it was supposed to tear them apart. This further proves that love can occur in the least expected situations. Lastly, I believe that sleep has some sort of symbolic meaning in this story. In this story's ending, the author writes, "As she emptied it of money, the bank filled with sleep." Obviously, everyone in the bank didn't fall asleep, so there must be a deeper meaning. I believe that the sleeping in this story is symbolic of unawareness. This is important because people often play dumb in order to escape danger. So, are the people in the bank pretending to be unaware? I believe so. I think that they are pretending to be unaware so that the robber doesn't go after them. It could also mean that sometimes you are unaware that you are being robbed. This can have a deeper meaning. Sometimes in relationships, you think your relationship is going great, but you're actually being robbed of something such as your independence. You aren't always aware that this is happening, but afterwards it becomes a problem. Essentially, I believe that danger=love and gun=love (even if it's toxic love). Then, together they create a child, which is symbolic to an outcome in real-life. If danger can be represented by love, and so can a gun, then together this shows that love can happen in the least expected times.

> Initial evidence for theme

> Meeting the goal of taking the analysis further, and showing how the author develops even deeper meaning within the theme. Dana identifies symbolism, and she shows two slight twists on the broader themes.

> Another example of Dana taking her analysis further to examine how the author crafts the theme's intricacies.

> Meeting her goal of showing how smaller aspects of the theme connect to create a broader understanding.

FIGURE 72. Round 3: Reading activity from Dana's ILP (excerpt).

After the last round of activities, students arrive at answers to their EQs while completing the third EQ reflection. This section allows students to revisit the progress they have made over the course of the unit, how much their questions have expanded or narrowed, and what their texts, activities, and personal experiences have done to shape their thinking. Dana captured her understandings in the excerpts from her EQ Reflection 3 in Figure 73. Dana saw how her questions and responses evolved over the course of the unit and then applied that learning to some of her own writing, as she described in the last few sentences of her reflection. Just as before, she still recognized new directions in which to take this knowledge, showing her understanding that learning does not stop at the moment an assignment is turned in; however, at this point, she had a satisfying response to her EQs.

> **EQ Reflection 3:**
>
> How do your texts and research answer your questions? How has this work impacted your writing? What do you still want to learn?
>
> In my last round of activities, my text and research were targeted to answer my questions. So, I picked a short story titled *The Bank Robbery*, to help me answer these questions. The main question I was answering during the analysis of this text was, "Do any of us escape the things we fear?" Through this activity I found out that we actually don't. This is because the teller was being robbed, and she was very afraid of the robber and his pistol. However, she ended up falling in love with the robber, and the pistol was their child; so, she didn't escape any of her fears. From this reading, I also found out that we fear the unfamiliar because we just don't know what to expect. She was afraid of the man and his gun, but in reality, he never had intentions of killing her. He just wanted to scare her. Therefore, the gun was feared by the woman because it represented the possibility of death. Activity 8 was a lot of reflecting on my reading and writing skills that I should have mastered throughout this unit. I prepared notes for the discussion, and I explained the ways in which my skills improved to fulfill the Advanced Proficient criteria of the rubric. My notes for this were on the back of the rubric that I turned in to be graded. Lastly, in Activity 9, I further answered the essential question: "Why do humans fear the unfamiliar?" To answer this question, I looked at the guiding questions I added during Activity 6, where I focused on whether or not death can be represented in not gory ways. I answered this question through my writing because I found out that a lack of knowledge could also be considered death. The students that I taught in Jordan were lacking knowledge and also lacking growth, which can be considered mental death. I created a sense of death in my story by explaining that uneducated children can also have death in their lives. By doing this, I answered the question of how to create a sense of uncanny in your writing. This also answered the question that the uncanny/death doesn't necessarily have to be something scary. In the short story I wrote, uncanny was a lack of knowledge and not something scary. In conclusion, through my last round of activities, I was able to find out that humans fear the unfamiliar because they are scared of unknown knowledge and that we don't escape fear, we often revolve our lives around it. Reading *The Bank Robbery*, has helped impact my writing because I learned how to write using structure as an effect. I included a time lapse in my story, as well as structurally organizing my paragraphs to enhance the meaning of the story. I still want to learn more about people's doubles in a more psychological manner. I feel like that sort of thing is very interesting, and I'd like to learn about it on a more scientific level.

FIGURE 73. EQ Reflection 3 from Dana's ILP (excerpts).

Dana's final standards reflection was just as impressive. She recognized not just a shift in a grade, but also a shift in the quality of her work. She pointed out specific areas in which she showed tremendous growth, and she evaluated those against the requirements of the rubric. Her self-awareness was possible because of the opportunities for formative practice and thoughtful reflection in each round of activities that came before. Dana's last few sentences took her learning a step even further (see Figure 74). She recognized that she needed to "hit every part of the rubric" and ask for help early on in the process. She also explained how she made strides in her own personal learning habits. Her concluding sentence, "I finally understood what I had previously been doing wrong," also demonstrates her realization that self-awareness is key to improvement.

What progress have you made towards your standards? What do you still need to learn?

As of the third round of activities, I personally feel like I have hit the Advanced Proficient section on all three rubrics. From the first to the second round of activities, I had made a great amount of progress. I was missing portions of the rubric in my first round, so in my second round of activities, I really focused on hitting every part of the rubric. In my third round of activities, I worked on perfecting my skills to the best of my ability. My reading and writing improved from the second round to the third round of activities. Between Activity 4 and Activity 7, I improved connections among themes, gave a longer/better summary. For the textual evidence, I explained how each piece of evidence is representative of one of the themes. I explained how the author's choices impacted the theme, and each other. I took it a step further this round, and focused on a harder story, harder themes, and symbolism. In Activity 9, my writing wasn't jumpy and it was very detailed. I focused very much on "showing" and not "telling" and being concise. I also added impactful dialogue to help me "show." I was very picky about word choice, and I spend A TON of time worrying about which words would sound better in my story. My strengths for reading are identifying sophisticated themes and summarizing texts. My writing strengths are organization, creating an effective plot, structure, precise language, leaving the reader with a message, completing the steps of the writing process, and correct spelling and punctuation. My previous goal towards my reading standard had been creating a detailed analysis of key points of the themes. I did this in my final round of activities by focusing in on the symbolism in the short story I analyzed. This entailed looking at the themes closely and analyzing why the author chose to present the themes the way he did. Before, I just never seemed to have gone in-depth with this. Additionally, my writing goal for the last round of activities was to use more dialogue, and while editing my story, I added many inner thoughts and dialogue between characters.

My major takeaways of this unit were that "showing" and not "telling" is super useful in getting your point across in a more interesting way, and that being concise in story-writing is very important because you always want your reader to be engaged. I believe that I mastered analyzing themes and connecting them to each other, organizing my writing in an intriguing way, using dialogue, effective word choice, and being able to reflect on what I have done well and what I have not. I fell short of my expectations in the first couple rounds of activities. I was in the B/C range in the first round of activities. I should have came to tutorial and asked for help so that I could have done better on them. I learned from my mistake, and asked for help come the last round, and that is one of the reasons why I think I ended up mastering the skills- I finally understood what I had previously been doing wrong.

FIGURE 74. Standards Reflection 3 from Dana's ILP.

"So what?"

As described in Chapter 8, the "So what?" element of an ILP demonstrates the student's most important takeaway of the unit for an appropriate, authentic audience. Dana's takeaway was more content related, focusing on a lesson that she learned as she explored her EQs. An excerpt from her rationale, shown in Figure 75, explains what Dana planned to do with all that she had learned. Dana provides an honest reflection of her improvement in both her content and skills abilities. Even more so, she applies her learning to a problem that she sees for her peers. Her innovative solution shows knowledge of her audience and uses outside skills from the technology world.

So What?: The Outcomes

Now that you've developed your skills, learned new information, and gained insights, what are you going to do? This final project should be influenced by the work you've completed these past few weeks.

- First, determine what the main lesson of this unit is. What is your take-away in terms of the texts, skills, and/or questions? This is completely up to you, so be honest.
- Then, decide who needs to know about what you've learned. Is there an important skill or lesson you want to share with others? Find an authentic audience and articulate why this person or group of people are the best audience for your lesson.
- Develop a rationale for your product in which you discuss how your work has inspired you. Using your texts and at least two of the Intelligences, explain what you'll do for your project in the space below.

My major takeaways of this unit were that "showing" and not "telling" is super useful in getting your point across in a more interesting way, and that being concise in story-writing is very important because you always want your reader to be engaged. I believe that I mastered analyzing themes and connecting them to each other, organizing my writing in an intriguing way, using dialogue, effective word choice, and being able to reflect on what I have done well and what I have not.

There is an extremely important lesson that I learned in this unit. I want to share with others that stepping out of your comfort zone is extremely important. I believe pre-teens and teens should be my target audience because these are the ages where kids care the most about other's opinions of them. It is vital that students think outside of the box, and challenge their minds to extents not previously reached by them.

For my project, I will create an app that sends children a meme of encouragement a day, to entice them to step out of their comfort zone. If they feel like they want to follow the out-of-the-box idea, they can then click on the meme, which would direct them to ways of fulfilling this idea. For example, one of my memes would be about trying something new that they are scared to do. The link would then suggest activities like cliff diving or skydiving. Then, there would be a little journal space for them to write how they achieved the meme and how they felt about their accomplishments. They would also get points every time they achieved the task.on another meme. I feel that this idea is very important- children need to understand that not being like everyone else, trying something new, and getting out of their comfort zones are all very important concepts. At this age, I feel that students are most prone to try and fit into the stereotypes of society. This leads children to be reserved. So, by using my app, students will be more inclined to venture out and try new things; students will break down the barricade of familiarity.

FIGURE 75. "So what?" rationale from Dana's ILP.

Assessing the ILP as a Whole

Because the ILP requires students to move beyond content knowledge and skills, it is important to assess student's learning habits as well as the process. Students will receive summative grades for the final round of activities in each skill area. These grades assess the products of an entire unit's worth of hard work and effort. The ILP rubric shown in Figure 76 provides a way to assess students' skills and learning habits as they move through their inquiries. Additionally, you can assess students throughout the process using a flowchart, allowing them to gauge their progress as they move along (see Figure 77). This provides important feedback throughout the ILP, not just at the end.

Inquiry Learning Plan Rubric			
Criteria	Advanced Proficient	Proficient	Developing
Questions AASL 1.1.3, 1.2.1, 4.2.2	Essential questions are broad and philosophical in nature; guiding questions are specific and helpful. Questions cover a wide range of form and purpose. Questions require synthesis of texts and personal experience or insight. Students takes initiative in developing and refining questions.	Essential questions are broad, but may lack depth; guiding questions are specific but may be disconnected from EQs. Question format and purpose varies, with some redundancy or unrelated aspects; questions require analysis of texts. Student develops question on own, but may rely on others for refinement.	Essential questions may be too simple or impersonal; few, if any, guiding questions. Questions are repetitive in form or purpose; questions require only basic research or understanding. Student relies on teacher or peers to develop questions.
Learning Activities AASL 1.4.3, 2.2.4, 4.1.8	Activities are aligned to standards that the student hasn't yet mastered. Thoughtfully and creatively fulfills all criteria. Each round of activities shows a clear progression from one to the next, demonstrates evidence of successful inquiry and supports the final assessment.	Activities are aligned to standards that the student hasn't mastered. Fulfills all criteria. Some aspects of learning plan may not support inquiry or final assessment. Learning progression may be unclear.	Not all aspects of unit plan completed. Activities unaligned to standards. A strong disconnect between learning plan, inquiry, and/or final assessment. Learning progression is unclear.
EQ Reflections AASL 1.1.1, 2.1.1, 2.3.1, 3.4.1	Student synthesizes texts by incorporating specific details from the works and real-world content to create an original argument in response to the essential question.	Student attempts to synthesize texts by making connections OR creating an overall response to the essential question; however, he/she does not use text evidence to support points or connections.	Reflection does not synthesize works and does not respond to the essential question. Reflection is more summary of key points than a blending of texts into a new idea.
Standards Reflections AASL 2.1.2, 2.4.3, 2.4.4, 4.1.6	Student accurately articulates abilities in skill areas, using evidence from activities to demonstrate the assessment. Sets realistic and challenging goals for further growth.	Student articulates abilities in skill areas, with some inaccuracy. Student uses vague or broad evidence from activities. Student sets goals, but they may not engender growth.	Student does not address all skill areas or may have inaccurate assessment. Reflection lacks evidence and goals for the next round.
Work Ethic AASL 1.1.9, 1.3.4	Student is actively engaged in learning, challenging oneself throughout the unit. Student is eager to develop knowledge and skills and share learning with teacher and classmates.	Student is engaged in learning, occasionally sharing knowledge, insights, or resources with teacher and classmates. Students may need occasional reminders to stay focused on coursework.	Student is detached from learning, often needing reminders to focus on coursework. Student may detract from others' learning.
Information Search Process and Inquiry AASL 1.1.4, 1.2.2, 1.4.2, 1.4.4	Student uses feedback to develop understanding. Student is able to overcome obstacles such as time constraints and missteps in a professional manner. Student is curious and solves problems by using resources available. Student takes responsibility for the accuracy of sources and information.	Student uses some feedback to develop ideas, but may not respond to feedback that challenges thinking. Student is reluctant to reach outside "comfort zone." Student relies on teacher for sources and information.	Student does not respond to feedback. Student is content to be lazy, setting easily achievable goals. This opportunity is totally lost on this individual. Student uses inaccurate information.

FIGURE 76. ILP rubric.

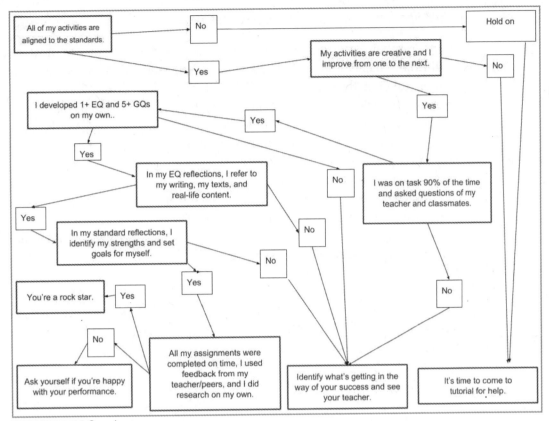

FIGURE 77. ILP flowchart.

Strategy: Assessing with the ILP Rubric

The ILP rubric in Figure 76 is similar to the habits rubric (see Figure 48). In addition to assessing work ethic and the ISP, we add criteria for questions, learning activities, and reflections. As with the habits rubric, our ILP rubric is based on the *Standards for the 21st Century Learner* (AASL, 2007, pp. 4, 5, 6, 7). It can be adapted based on your goals for your students by deleting the aspects of learning that students are not developing on their own; for example, if they are not choosing their own standards or creating their own activities, then leave out the portion that says, "Activities are aligned to standards that the student hasn't mastered." We use this rubric for a final summative grade at the end of each unit; it is also helpful to use formatively as check-ins along the way.

Strategy: ILP Flowchart for Self-Assessment

Another option for assessing the ILP is to use flowcharts, similar to those we outlined in Chapter 6. We mostly use these to help students reflect on how well they are fulfilling the requirements of the ILP; they are an excellent tool for conferences and help us to aid students in identifying misconceptions about the ILP or establishing new habits to help them find success. We ordered the flowchart depicted in Figure 77 in a way that prioritizes activities over questions and reflections, because, in our minds, activities are where students work most closely with knowledge and skills. Some of these requirements are unique to the needs of a course. Also, we wrote the final points of the flowchart in ways that reflect what we want our students to do next. The two bottom-right endpoints require students to meet with us to set goals. The next possible endpoint has students ask themselves if they are happy with their performance; this is a great talking point during a conference. Sometimes it's okay for students to decide that they are working as hard as they want to and that they are satisfied with the outcome, but we can use this time to point out strategies that will help them improve. Finally, the last endpoint at the bottom left celebrates their hard work and resulting progress.

What Does This Look Like in the Classroom?

Chapter 10 delves into several aspects of how the ILP plays out in the classroom. From the changing role of the teacher to the importance of reinforcing habits of mind like embracing the messiness of learning, this chapter provides insight into strategies that may be absent in a traditional classroom setting. Strategies such as celebrating successes and resisting micromanaging are crucial to the process. Several pitfalls are addressed as well, particularly related to students feeling overwhelmed by a new way of learning and even jealous of those who are learning in more familiar and comfortable ways. Last, the chapter provides options for how the ILP "lives" in the classroom in either print or digital forms.

Strategy: Becoming a Facilitator

Using the ILP creates a different type of classroom structure because it is dictated by student need and is therefore variable. In this structure, you take on a facilitator role; at the core of facilitation is asking questions. You will be engaged in conferencing one on one, circulating around the room reminding students of the rubric requirements, monitoring student groups, gauging how students are feeling, doing full-class or small-group mini-lessons, and helping students in whatever way is needed at that moment. You become a coach, mentor, cheerleader, and guide.

Because your role involves responding more than leading, students have more control of what and how they learn. Student takeaways can range from an understanding of purposeful diction and syntax in argument writing to recognizing how to collaborate with and learn from others. At the start of the unit, you cannot predict every takeaway a student will have. Rather, your ability to react to each individual's needs will shape a unique experience with unique results.

Erin Sollner, a special education teacher, works as an in-class support teacher in a high school English classroom. After her first team-teaching experience with

Cathy using the ILP, she described her role as "facilitator" during an interview. She said a teacher fills this role by:

> observing student needs and then responding.... It's a very responsive role. You have to be gauging what your students' needs are and then act accordingly ... as opposed to planning it all out. You give a framework for what they need and you provide certain expectations ... and lessons ... but what you do after you've set it all up is all about responding to what they need, giving an enormous amount feedback.... There's so much interaction with the teacher. (Sollner, 2014)

Erin also quickly recognized one of the ILP's benefits:

> This type of education embeds some of the basic tenets of special education because it's individualized. It inherently meets the needs of the IEP [a student's individualized education program, which is enforceable by law in New Jersey]. ... In some ways, it reflects exactly what an IEP is intended for—to individualize instruction. And that is what's happening when you're having students do this, go through this process, so, in terms of modifications, you're doing it. (Sollner, 2012)

 Every day in class is customized by the students and the teacher to best meet the needs and goals of each student. To see a sample in-class support student's work, please refer to Dan's ILP in the online appendix.

Strategy: Reinforcing the Messiness of Learning

We make sure to focus on how learning to learn is so much more important than being told what to learn. As we explained in the introduction, this lack of explicit direction from the teacher is initially a source of frustration; however, students eventually see the value. Michelle, a senior, wrote in her final class reflection:

> Using the ILP taught me about every stage of the learning process. It was a whole new concept than anything I had done in a class before. It took a while to get used to, but, by the end of the class, I really appreciated the ILP because it gave us students the freedom to explore topics that interested us, and move at our own pace of learning.

Therefore, it is so important to work through the first unit as slowly as possible with loads of opportunities for interventions. Let students experience it together so they have a common bond—even if that bond is based on their frustration! As students develop the skills on their own, they become resources and cheerleaders for the rest of the class. Without a doubt, we have always had students like these, who revel in the opportunity and encourage others throughout the process.

We often hear about the frustrations and the breakthroughs while reading student reflections. Nolan, an eleventh grader, explained his evolution in his British Literature class:

> [At the end of the first unit,] I was still very skeptic[al] about The Inquiry Process, but . . . kicking and screaming, I kept my head down and pushed forward. . . . The journey began to get to me mentally.

Nolan's skepticism stemmed from his frustrations with finding answers to his questions in the first two units and connecting to the texts in a personally meaningful way. As a student in a first block class, Nolan always arrived with coffee and criticism in hand. But, by working closely with his peers and teacher and using his reflections to voice his experience with the learning process, he pushed himself through:

> After I broke through that stubbornness and teenage angst of [high school,] I really began to come up with some quality inquiries. In the back of my mind, I had that idea of religion still locked into my mind but it was during this period, I really started to see men believe that they are more than God. In *Frankenstein*, the doctor attempts to create life from death, and this leads to his untimely demise. From this, I formed the question "How dangerous is humanity's thirst for knowledge?" and through this question I ran into some issues. In my first reflections, I found that this question was scratching just the surface. So I started thinking, *what has been a constant through all of the units?* Change. Change has been the common thread that has held together all of British literature. The poem "If" by Rudyard Kipling offers advice to not change, but in *Frankenstein*, no one accepts the monster because of its very existence. And then I had a breakthrough; the world was not ready for the Renaissance's ideas but it accepted them, the world was not ready to be propelled into the next era but it was and over time, these changes became generally accepted.

It took Nolan two solid units to finally embrace the process, but, in turn, he had a breakthrough with his questions. In fact, he noted in his final course reflection that "every single time period funneled me closer and closer to my answer, and

I will always be in debt to this class for that." Each student is going to have a different turning point, so it is important that you are checking in often with each of them to see where they are in the process.

Strategy: Scaffolding the ILP

Though the end goal of the ILP is to give students control over their learning, there are ways to scaffold letting go of the various aspects of the plan. As mentioned in previous chapters, just as you can give over control of only questions or rubrics without using the ILP, scaffolding can be done when using the ILP over several units as well. In fact, if students are unfamiliar with inquiry, standards, or any of the other core concepts of this plan, we recommend that you begin the course by designing some aspects of the ILP and slowly giving students more responsibility over time.

In Meg's Honors Imaginative Process class, students complete four different units, with varying levels of control over each. Figure 78 provides an overview of this scaffolding, and each unit is further detailed below. During the first unit, in which students study poetry and the creative process, students practice all the same standards and have the same overarching EQs: "What is art?" and "What is the creative process and its relevance to reality?" The class develops a list of GQs together and students choose from that master list; some of the activities are designed by Meg and some are designed by students in inquiry groups. Students read some poems as a class and can choose a long text from a pre-approved list that is studied in inquiry groups. To allow for choice, students

	Unit 1	Unit 2	Unit 3	Unit 4
Texts	Mostly teacher Some student	Some teacher Some student	One teacher Mostly student	All student
Questions	EQ: Teacher GQ: Student	EQ: Student GQ: Student	EQ: Student GQ: Student	EQ: Student GQ: Student
Standards	Teacher	Teacher	Teacher	Student
Activity Design	Teacher	Mostly teacher Some student	One teacher Mostly student	Student
Rubric Creation	All teacher	Mostly teacher 1 student (reading)	1 teacher (writing) 2 student (reading and speaking)	All student, except for ILP

FIGURE 78. Unit overview from an Honors Imaginative Process class, illustrating the gradual release of responsibility and choice to students.

choose an individual book of poetry from which they will select ten poems to analyze independently.

During the second unit, the focus of which is on short stories and the uncanny, students are again practicing the same skills as their peers. Similar to the first unit, students have a list of texts to choose from, but this time the list offers more than twenty choices, rather than six; additionally, students have free rein over choosing short stories and microfiction for study. Though Meg still offers some selections for the class to study, students also begin to choose resources to support their inquiry. For example, all students read Sigmund Freud's essay "The Uncanny" to help them create their own EQs and GQs. Because students are taking more control of their learning experience, they also start to design their own activities. (For more on this unit, see Dana's plan, excerpts of which are shown in Chapter 9 and which is presented in full in the online appendix.)

Students write scripts in the third unit and read the pilot script of the television show *Lost* (Abrams & Lindelof, 2004) to study structure; this is the only text students read as a class during this unit. The rest are self-selected. The class continues to practice the same standards, but they again have full control over the questions. Meg designs the first activity to set students up for the unit, but the students then work in inquiry groups or by themselves to design the remaining activities.

By the final unit of the year, students are wholly responsible for text and standard selection, question creation, standard selection, and activity design and completion. As illustrated in Figure 78, students have slowly taken control over aspects of learning that are typically decided by the teacher. It helps to decide

Pitfall: Feeling Overwhelmed

Even with scaffolding and a gradual release of control, some students feel that there is not enough guidance when using a class structure such as this. Liz, a junior, wrote that she:

> often felt more lost and confused [than] I was excited or organized. I think that it is difficult to create a whole ILP and activities from a completely blank slate. I am the type of student that likes to know what I have to do, when I have to do it, and how it should be done. However, the creativity aspect of being able to have control over what I learned was more beneficial to my learning.

This speaks to what we've discussed in previous chapters, that students are familiar and comfortable with the teacher directing every move they make. Though some students may struggle with the structure of the plan and its emphasis on freedom and student responsibility, we make sure they know that everybody struggles when they encounter a new experience that makes them feel uneasy. Reminding students that the ISP (see Figure 2) normalizes these feelings of uncertainty and confusion as simply part of the process is key to helping students through the discomfort that can arise during inquiry. As one eleventh-grade student noted in an anonymous end-of-course reflection:

> At first everything is going to seem very confusing and unclear, but like Carol Kuhlthau says "we need to go through a period of uncertainty before we can earn clarity and a sense of accomplishment!" And trust me; it happened to all of us in the class.

how you want to release control to students, and this decision should be based on your curriculum. If there are certain texts or concepts that we are required to cover, we usually study them earlier in the year.

Strategy: Celebrating Successes

When we first began using the ILP, students were frustrated in class—a couple of students began to voice complaints, and, before we knew it, we had a classroom full of angsty students criticizing our teaching methods. This happens when we open up the field of learning to them—they develop their voices and they actually use them now that it's "our classroom." Therefore, it is so important to move the spotlight from the teaching methods and back onto them and their accomplishments; accentuate the positive and show them how much they have changed. For example, we have compared students' first activities to their current ones to show growth. We have also shared with the class how proud we are of their insightful questions and reflections. Jeanine Brown, a teacher at Whittier Christian High School in California, began using the ILP after attending one of our sessions at the NCTE Annual Convention. She shared her celebration experience with us:

> I have already incorporated a few of your ideas, most notably "celebrating" success, and that had a huge impact on my students. One girl articulated that she has been so focused on the negatives that she hadn't even noticed her growth until I asked her to consider it. They have been doing reflections, but this was zoomed in on progress. It has been exciting to have them identify benefits of this unit and style of instruction, such as improved problem-solving, organization of thought, evaluation of sources, and internet research. (Personal communication, February 26, 2014)

When working with the ILP, students realize all that goes into learning—it is about so much more than content and standards! Students have learned to work within a traditional school system and have expected a traditional outcome, so it takes time and proof to show them how the new system succeeds.

Enthusiasm for education is a similar and equally important tool for celebration. We need to communicate our pride in our work and our genuine interest in helping our students discover new learning. As a young teacher, Meg was often criticized by her students for not running her class the same way as other English teachers in the school. She met their refrain "We're the only class in this school that does this!" with "Yeah! Isn't that awesome? You're pioneers!" Cathy even called her class the "American Lit Adventure" and Meg called hers the "Brit Lit Pilgrimage—to Learning"! Transparency is important and helps to build trust between the teacher and students; this may be new to them, but it is a system that we have been practicing for years.

Strategy: Resisting Micromanagement

Turning over the control of learning to students doesn't suddenly mean that teaching becomes an easy job where you get to just sit back with your feet up. But this approach shouldn't be more difficult than a teacher-centered classroom—it's just *different*. When we first started teaching this way, we were definitely overwhelmed! We felt the need to assess everything students produced since they were in control of their learning process and we didn't know how it would turn out for them. But, having used these strategies for many years now, we know how successful students are with them, and we have also developed a few ways to manage our own time, many of which are detailed in previous chapters. For example:

- To help you manage the workflow, students need to keep their ILPs updated. If you have chosen the standards, you know what they are, but it still helps for them to be listed on the ILP. If they have chosen the standards, it is even more important for them to be listed so you know what to assess when you evaluate an activity.

- Ask that your students write their standards on the activity itself and reiterate their EQs in their reflections. Those seconds scrolling or flipping to the front page count!

- Build in a few minutes at the end of each class or week for students to update questions, so that you can quickly see where their thinking is headed.

- Encourage students to provide context for their reading and thinking. Because they may be reading a text that you haven't read, students must give enough information in their activities and reflections to provide you or a peer with an understanding of the text. This is standard practice in literary analysis, but it becomes crucial when each student is reading different texts.

- Ask students to identify specific areas that need to be addressed by annotating or highlighting their work. This should occur before you give students feedback.

- Ask your students to fill out rubrics for their activities and turn those in, or, if working in an online platform, they can paste their rubrics directly into their activities. That way, when you assess by responding to their self-assessment, you can give advice specific to their needs. Use the same rubric for self-assessments.

- Use annotated activities, rubrics, and reflections that demonstrate areas for growth as the basis for student-led conferences the next day.

- Use workshop time for formative assessment and feedback. Five minutes of one-on-one time can be more beneficial than you spending fifteen minutes leaving them notes, but make sure they are recording the feedback you give them!

- Create peer review experiences for students who are working on similar standards. Have them annotate one another's work, using language from the rubrics or standards. This helps you focus your feedback, but it also gives you another approach to assessing skills: seeing if the editor is providing meaningful feedback.

How the ILP Lives in Your Classroom: Paper or Digital?

Students aren't used to seeing the various organizational tools that teachers use to map curriculum and daily lesson plans, so being confronted with a document like the ILP that will guide an entire unit can feel overwhelming. Depending on your school's technology access, there are different approaches to presenting the plan and to help you and your students navigate it.

Physical

For many teachers, having a physical copy of the ILP is going to be the only approach. A sheet that has the "What I will read" and "What I will learn" sections can serve as an introduction of sorts; usually a student can fit these two categories on both sides of a sheet of paper. We will put this at the front of a folder so that students can place activity sheets behind it. It is helpful for students to have a table of contents on the inside cover where they list the names of the activities in the order they appear. When the ILP is physical, we give the students sheets with the reflection prompts so that they can easily refer to the questions when writing (see the online appendix). Finally, students will have a copy of the "So what?" directions to accompany their rationale. Keeping all of the documents in one folder or binder keeps students organized; the folder can also be reviewed at the end of the unit in order for students to receive an ILP grade.

Pitfall: Student Time Management

No matter the class, students will struggle with managing their time—it's often a part of the struggle of being a teen! However, the ILP can present particular problems when it comes to time management. Because students are completing activities that may be different from their peers, it can be difficult for them to meet deadlines with such individualized work. Until students get the hang of the process, they sometimes think an activity can be done in a night like other homework assignments. Standards do not cover just one skill, so activities often have multiple parts. Therefore, we have to focus our attention on time management and make sure to give students deadlines, as most teachers do with large projects or essays. The main goal is to help them begin to manage their own time by analyzing their desired outcomes, creating a project timeline to meet it, and learning how to alter that timeline as needed. Often, we will meet with our students right after they design their activities to discuss when they will practice each part; we guide them to set mini-deadlines for themselves. This saves both us and them a headache.

We also make sure they are getting plenty of workshop time in class to practice skills and complete reflections while the teacher is in the room to help; this allows us to conference with them too and catch any issues quickly. Conferencing, as discussed in Chapter 6, is a crucial aspect of this approach, and it plays a big role in time management. It allows us to gauge where the students are in the process and to adjust and encourage accordingly.

It's also important to allow time at the beginning of a unit, perhaps more so than in other classes. Students may have many initial questions, so they need to be reminded to do some preliminary searching before they decide on a topic. Kuhlthau et al.'s (2012) *Guided Inquiry Design: A Framework for Inquiry in Your School* suggests that students consider the following four criteria: "What is interesting to me? What are my learning goals? How much information is available? How much time do I have?" (pp. 96–97). This allows them to figure out what is feasible and what they can reasonably accomplish over the course of a unit.

Obviously, time is not limitless, so determine an absolute cut-off date for students who need a little extra time to get started. We've had students walk out of the library with a stack of books they want to explore, and, though we wish they could pursue all these lines of learning, we need to give a deadline. Therefore, they will have time to determine the scope of what they want to accomplish, leading them to eventually set their own deadlines. If they are still uncertain as to what they want to pursue because there are so many options of interest, perhaps they can be paired up with someone in the class studying a similar topic—the students could split up ideas or even pursue the counterargument. The hardest part is starting, so we want to give them the tools to learn what they need to get going. Eventually, as Meg does with her juniors and seniors, you can give them a final unit in which they begin on their own, using all that they've learned to start well and recover when things go awry.

Electronic: Google Drive and Google Classroom

Over the last few years, our school has transitioned to using the Google platform for much of our work, and creating a Google Doc for the ILP is an excellent marriage. It allows students to access one document with all of their work so that they can easily refer back to previous reflections or activities. Using Google Drive is both an advantage and a burden—when students complete everything in one document, an ILP can grow upwards of thirty pages. Students may want to complete each activity on a separate Google Doc and then link the activities back to their ILP document (see Figure 79). This helps students with the visual aspect of the ILP, which can seem monstrous when they try to scroll through a document to find the particular activity or reflection they are working on.

When we use Google Drive, we use the Table of Contents feature, which allows the user to link to various spots in the document (see Figure 80). This makes it easy for both you and your students to jump from the top of the document to any activity or reflection. Google Drive also allows the user to view

Activity 1:   My activity one is handwritten but I took a picture of it and the document is below.   Venn Diagram Picture
Activity 2:   Annotations   5 Rules of Microfiction   Microfiction
Activity 3:   Brainstorming
EQ Reflection: How do your texts and research answer your questions? How has your reading and research impacted your writing? What do you still want to learn?   EQ Reflection 1
Standards Reflection: What progress have you made towards your standards? What do you still need to learn about these skills? Refer to the standards specifically.   Standards Reflection 2

FIGURE 79. ILP with links to activities and reflections. CC BY-NC-SA. AASL standards excerpted from *Standards for the 21st Century Learner* (AASL, 2007, 4, 5, 6, 7).

an outline on the side of the document (see Figure 81). This is especially helpful when students are completing reflections and referring to multiple activities.

Usually, we create a master ILP to share with the students and then they make copies to populate for themselves, but recently Google has created Google Classroom, which allows the teacher to create one document that then makes a copy for each student. This way, we can be sure students have named the document something identifiable and we know for sure that we can easily access it through Google Classroom. Classroom also allows students to "turn in" an assignment; we have used this feature both for when students are ready to receive a final grade and when they need formative feedback.

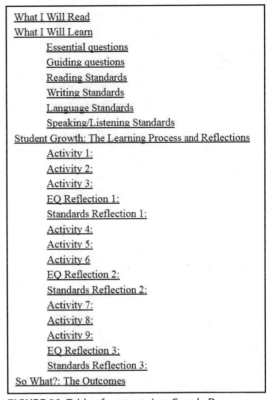

FIGURE 80. Table of contents in a Google Doc.

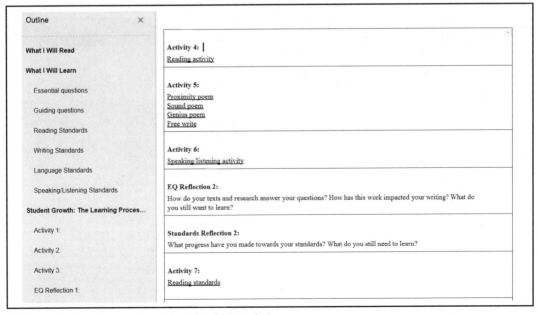

FIGURE 81. Table of contents on the side of a Google Doc.

Electronic: Websites

One final approach is to create a website for the ILP (see Figure 82). The ILP is still separated into its various components and is arranged linearly, but it allows the students some creativity in how they decorate and share their page. Our sample shown in Figure 82 uses Google Sites, but any platform that you are familiar with would work. This idea came about when Meg and Cathy were learning about ePortfolios, so, if your school is undertaking a similar initiative, the ILP could serve as one approach. We encourage you to be flexible with the format of the plan, but we remind students it is their responsibility to keep their materials organized and neat in a way that will be easy for you to find and assess materials.

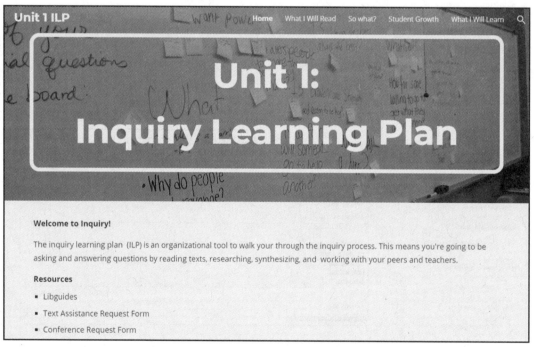

FIGURE 82. ILP website created with Google Sites.

11

The ILP as a Flexible Tool for Inquiry

Of course, we recognize that the requirements of each teacher and each course are unique, so we encourage anyone who uses the ILP to adapt it as needed. This offers the flexibility of using some but not all of the ILP's elements, and it provides an opportunity to scaffold the "letting go" process. ILPs are most commonly used in English classes as unit plans. However, it has been adapted by English teachers and by teachers of other disciplines for projects and course-long plans. We share these variations below, from the most teacher-directed to the most student-designed adaptations.

An ILP for Gender Studies

As other teachers have adopted the plan, they made changes to the structure, like putting the standards or questions before texts because that is what worked for their curricular approach. Often, teachers who are attempting the plan for the first time use it for only one unit and therefore choose the aspects of the plan they feel are most important for their course. Lindsay Warren, a social studies teacher, adapted the plan for a unit in her Gender Studies class as outlined in Figure 83. Because her students would work through this process only once, she required specific activities and standards but allowed for individualization in questions and resources. She also assessed students using the AASL standards listed in Figure 83 and had them complete a "So what?" section. Lindsay chose to maintain control over standards and activities, but she let go of the decision making when it came to inquiry questions, texts, and products.

An ILP for Genius Hour

Meg adapted the ILP to use during "genius hour" (Kesler, 2016), inspired by Google's initiative for their employees to spend 20 percent of their time on passion projects of their own design. Juliani (2014) and Kesler, as well as other edu-

Gender Studies Inquiry Learning Plan
The Starting Point: Resources
List resources below that will aid your inquiry. (This list will expand throughout the process.)
What I Will Learn?
Please list your essential and guiding questions that you plan on pursuing throughout this course.   **Essential question/s:**   **Guiding questions:**
Student Growth: The Learning Process and Reflections
Learning Activities: Throughout the unit, you will complete six activities. By the end of the unit, you will be synthesizing what you've learned about gender studies to help you better understand your essential questions, and all of the standards will be addressed in the activities.
Activity 1: Binaries PowerPoint   *Reflection:*   *What questions do you have?*
Activity 2: Blank Slate PowerPoint   *Reflection:*   *What questions do you have?*
Activity 3: Gender Sources Databases & Discussion   *Reflection:*
Content Reflection: How does your research relate to each other and to historical, contemporary, or personal examples? What questions can you generate from your research?
Standards Reflection: What progress have you made toward the standards? What do you still need to learn (regarding the standards)?
Activity 4: Exploratory Survey   *Reflection:*
Activity 5: Creating Inquiry Questions   *Reflection:*
Activity 6: Source Compilation & Evaluation   *Reflection:*
Essential Question Reflection: How does your research relate to each other and to historical, contemporary, or personal examples? How does your work answer your questions?
Standards Reflection: What progress have you made toward your standards? What do you still need to learn (regarding the standards)?

FIGURE 83. Gender Studies ILP. Reproduced with permission from Lindsay Warren. AASL standards excerpted from *Standards for the 21st Century Learner* by the American Association of School Librarians, a division of the American Library Association, copyright © 2007 American Library Association. Used with permission.

FIGURE 83. Continued.

So What?: The Outcomes
Now that you've developed your skills, learned new information, and gained insights, what are you going to do? This final project should be influenced by the work you've completed these past several weeks.

- First, determine what the main lesson of this inquiry project is. What is your take-away in terms of the resources, standards, and essential questions? Then, decide who needs to know about what you've learned. Is there an important lesson or a few insights you want to share with others? Find an authentic audience and articulate why this person or group of people are the best audience for your lesson. What means will you use to communicate your discoveries?
- Develop a rationale/proposal for your project in which you'll discuss how your work has inspired you. Using your resources and standards, explain what you'll do for your project in the Inquiry Project Proposal.
- Finally, create the product which you've outlined in your rationale/proposal and share it with your audience!

American Association of School Librarians Standards
1.1.1: Follow an inquiry-based process in seeking knowledge in curricular subjects, and make the real world connection for using this process in own life.
1.1.3: Develop and refine a range of questions to frame the search for new understanding
1.1.4: Find, evaluate, and select appropriate sources to answer questions.
1.1.9: Collaborate with others to broaden and deepen understanding
1.2.5: Demonstrate adaptability by changing the inquiry focus, questions, resources, or strategies when necessary to achieve success.
1.4.2: Use interaction with and feedback from teachers and peers to guide own inquiry process.
2.2.4: Demonstrate personal productivity by completing products to express learning.

cators, have developed lots of useful resources for genius hour, and Meg saw an opportunity to use the ILP to keep students organized throughout their genius hour time.

The first two sections of the genius hour ILP (or "GHILP," as Meg's students call it) are different from the generic ILP; students spend two or three classes brainstorming ideas for their passion project and having it vetted by their classmates, so the first section of the genius hour ILP requires students to write up a summary of what they hope for their project (see Figure 84). The next section has students determine what they already know about their topic, including any skills they have that might be useful. This is like a KWL (know–wonder–learn) chart.

Once students have begun exploring their topic, they complete the "What I will learn" section, which is pulled directly from the generic ILP. Here, students list questions they have developed in class, but they also list the skills they will need to successfully complete their project. These skills are likely not standards; they might include items such as "learn how to change my car's oil" or "learn how to make pasta." However, Meg also included the standards she knew her students would be practicing as part of the research and presentation project (see Figure 85).

Genius Hour
Write a summary of your genius hour project. What do you hope to accomplish? Why do you want to do this?

What I Know Now
What I can do now: What I know now:

FIGURE 84. Project information and "What I know now" from the genius hour ILP.

What I Will Learn
List your questions below:
List the skills you will need below:

-
-
-
- CCSS.ELA-LITERACY.RI.11-12.7: Integrate and evaluate multiple sources of information presented in different media or formats (e.g., visually, quantitatively) as well as in words in order to address a question or solve a problem.
- CCSS.ELA-LITERACY.W.11-12.7: Conduct short as well as more sustained research projects to answer a question (including a self-generated question) or solve a problem; narrow or broaden the inquiry when appropriate; synthesize multiple sources on the subject, demonstrating understanding of the subject under investigation.
- CCSS.ELA-LITERACY.W.11-12.8: Gather relevant information from multiple authoritative print and digital sources, using advanced searches effectively; assess the strengths and limitations of each source in terms of the task, purpose, and audience; integrate information into the text selectively to maintain the flow of ideas, avoiding plagiarism and overreliance on any one source and following a standard format for citation. (MLA).
- CCSS.ELA-LITERACY.SL.11-12.2: Integrate multiple sources of information presented in diverse media or formats (e.g., visually, quantitatively, qualitatively, orally) evaluating the credibility and accuracy of each source.
- CCSS.ELA-LITERACY.SL.11-12.4: Present information, findings and supporting evidence clearly, concisely, and logically. The content, organization, development, and style are appropriate to task, purpose, and audience.
- CCSS.ELA-LITERACY.SL.11-12.5: Make strategic use of digital media (e.g., textual, graphical, audio, visual, and interactive elements) in presentations to enhance understanding of findings, reasoning, and evidence and to add interest.
- CCSS.ELA-LITERACY.SL.11-12.6: Adapt speech to a variety of contexts and tasks, demonstrating a command of formal English when indicated or appropriate.
- AASL.1.1.3: Develop and refine a range of questions to frame the search for new understanding.
- AASL.1.1.4: Find, evaluate, and select appropriate sources to answer questions.

FIGURE 85. "What I will learn" from the genius hour ILP. AASL standards excerpted from *Standards for the 21st Century Learner* by the American Association of School Librarians, a division of the American Library Association, copyright © 2007 American Library Association. Used with permission. CCSS excerpted from CCSSI (2010).

Resources
During your Genius Hour time, you will be researching your topic. This research could include articles, videos, podcasts, social media, Wikipedia entries, visits to important/useful places, etc. You are not limited to ten sources, but it is a good starting point.   1.   2.   3.   4.   5.   6.   7.   8.   9.   10.   Additionally, you will interview an expert on your topic. List the name of your interviewee and the date and location the interview occurred below: •   Interviewee: •   Date: •   Location:

FIGURE 86. "Resources" from the genius hour ILP.

Throughout the genius hour time, students will also be listing their resources. This takes the place of the "What I will read" section of the generic ILP, since students will rarely start with a text. Meg also requires her students to interview an expert, so that is listed under resources as well (see Figure 86).

Because Meg's students work on their genius hour every fifth class period for the entire school year, the activity boxes are replaced by "session" boxes in the "Student growth" section. Additionally, students complete a reflection after most sessions, rather than after every three activities. The first seven of eighteen sessions are outlined in Figure 87. Once students have completed the learning and research for their genius hour project, they complete the "So what?" project, explaining their biggest takeaway as well as how their year-long inquiry led them to that conclusion.

Student Growth: The Learning Process and Reflections
Learning Activities: Throughout your Genius Hour time, you will learn about your topic, including the skills and knowledge necessary to produce an artifact of your learning.
Session 1   •   Complete "What is Your Passion?"
Session 2   •   Complete proposal and have class discuss it

FIGURE 87. "Student growth" from the genius hour ILP.

continued on p. 180

FIGURE 87. Continued.

Session 3
•   Develop questions.
•   Update Learning Plan.
•   Begin researching, if possible.
•   Complete reflection.
Reflection: Write at least 200 words in response to the following questions:
•   What are you most excited about for this project?
•   What are you most worried about?
•   How can your teacher and classmates help you?
•   Were you able to start researching? If not, why not?
•   What is your next step? What will you work on next class?
Session 4
• Review keywords powerpoint
• Brainstorm a list of search terms.
o Choose one or two of your questions as an essential question.
o Develop **twenty** new search terms.
■ EBSCO
■ Thesaurus.com
■ Sample
• Review Google Advanced Search options
• Find at least two credible sources.
• Take notes on each. For each source, complete a source sheet and place a link in your ILP under Resources.
• Complete today's reflection.
Reflection: Write at least 200 words in response to the following questions:
• What did you accomplish today?
• What search terms did you use?
• Which terms were most successful? Which were least successful? Why?
• What is the most interesting thing you learned today? Why?
• What is your next step? What will you work on next class?
Session 5
Research
• Using the keywords that you developed last Genius Hour, you have 15 minutes to find a credible, useful source.
o Use Google Advanced Search or one of the databases
o You can also review your questions to guide your searching.
o Keep the source open in a tab on your Chromebook.
Sharing Protocol
• Meet with your assigned partner.
o Each of you will explain to the other what your Genius Hour project is.
o What is your goal? What is one of your main questions?
• Then, switch resources with your partner (switch chromebooks). Complete the "Peer Source Evaluation" sheet.
• Finally, share your answers with your peer
Return to research
• Using the feedback from your partner, as well as your keywords and questions, find a second resource in 10 minutes.
Sharing Protocol
• Meet with any partner you wish but not the assigned partner from before.
o Each of you will explain to the other what your Genius Hour project is.
o What is your goal? What is one of your main questions?
• Then, switch resources with your partner (switch chromebooks). Complete the "Peer Source Evaluation" sheet.
• Finally, share your answers with your peer
Note-taking
• Take notes on each. For each source, complete a source sheet (on *Google Classroom*) and place a link in your ILP under Resources.
• You can use the feedback from your partner.
Reflection
• In your GHILP, write a response to the following questions:
• How did your partners help you today?
• Considering your research efforts, source selections, and source work with a peer, evaluate yourself as a researcher and source evaluator. What are your strengths? In what ways can you improve?
• What is your next step? What will you work on next class? What do you need help with?

An ILP for Holocaust Studies

Dan Butler, a social studies teacher, adapted the generic ILP to be a template for an inquiry study of the Nazis' remaking of society in World War II Germany. Knowing that he wanted the "So what?" section to be a full-class discussion, Dan had to control the EQ as well. That way, no matter where students' inquiries took them, they would be able to share their findings in meaningful ways at the end of the unit. He began with this EQ: "How are the Nazis able to create the society needed to foster their goal of a totalitarian state?"

He also maintained control of the unit's standards, so the "What I will learn" section of his ILP was complete when the students received it (see Figure 88). Dan required that students choose two of the three standards he adapted from state and Common Core standards.

What I Will Learn
Choose two of the following standards that you will address in this project:
Integrate information from diverse sources, both primary and secondary, into a coherent understanding of an idea or event in order to determine the factors that contributed to the totalitarian takeover of Germany by the Nazis.
Students will evaluate authors' differing points of view on the same historical event or issue by assessing the authors' claims, reasoning, and evidence in order to discuss the social, economic, and political conditions that contributed to the totalitarian takeover of Germany by the Nazis.
Determine the central ideas or information of a primary or secondary source; provide an accurate summary that makes clear the relationships among the key details and ideas the author expresses that contributed to the totalitarian takeover of Germany by the Nazis.

FIGURE 88. "What I will learn" from the Holocaust studies ILP. Reproduced with permission from Dan Butler.

He then suggested several formats the students could explore (e.g., artwork, speeches, propaganda, etc.), and he allowed them to choose texts within those mediums. They listed their core and supplementary resources in a section he called "What I will research and where" (see Figure 89). As students began reading and evaluating their sources and he began talking with them about the things they were learning, he realized he needed to provide a space for them to track additional, follow-up questions that individualized their explorations further. He added space for those in this section as well.

What I will research and where
Topic:
List the core materials below.
List resources below that will aid your inquiry.
Sub questions:

FIGURE 89. "What I will research and where" from the Holocaust studies ILP. Reproduced with permission from Dan Butler.

Because his class only meets for half of the year, and he was more pressed for time, Dan only did two rounds of activities, but he still recognized the importance of reflection after each round. He provided formative feedback on Activities 1 and 2, and then he graded Activities 3 and 4 (see Figure 90).

Student Growth: The Learning Process and Reflections
Learning Activities: Throughout the course of this unit, you will complete four activities. By the end of the unit, you will be synthesizing what you've learned about your texts and research to help you better understand your essential questions, and all of the standards must be addressed at least twice in the activities. You will also be sharing the information you learn about Nazi Germany with your classmates
Activity 1:
Activity 2:
EQ Reflection: How do your texts and research relate to each other and to other knowledge you had of your chosen topic? How does your work answer your questions?
Standards Reflection: What progress have you made toward your standards? What do you still need to learn?
Activity 3:
Activity 4:
EQ Reflection: How do your texts and research relate to each other and to other knowledge you had of your chosen topic? How does your work answer your questions?
Standards Reflection: What progress have you made toward your standards? What do you still need to learn?

FIGURE 90. "Student growth" from the Holocaust studies ILP. Reproduced with permission from Dan Butler.

After those two rounds of activities and reflections, Dan's students prepared for a discussion in which they could share all they learned. In the ILP, he provided the instructions shown in Figure 91. The questions in the first bullet point ask students to share information they found but also to discuss the inquiry and research processes and what they learned about themselves. The second two bullet points ask them to reflect on the information relayed by their peers and synthesize all of it to determine what the class knows about Nazi Germany because of these processes. They also need to evaluate what information they're missing for the third bullet point. These are difficult skills, for sure, but, as Dan reported, students felt prepared to discuss these aspects because of the tremendous amount of thought that had gone into the unit prior to that final day.

Dan's version of the ILP demonstrates a blend of letting go and maintaining control. His curriculum was slightly more prescribed, but he did see room for student choice in the texts and in the activities. After his first attempt at the inquiry process, he knew immediately that he wanted to turn over even more responsibility to the students, and he began talking with his fellow subject area teachers and his supervisor about providing more flexibility.

While adapting the plan, consider where you need to maintain control and where you can encourage student choice. We have seen numerous variations of the process in this way. When we asked where those new to inquiry should start, a history teacher talked about starting small. Basically, decide what is nonnegotiable and where you feel comfortable allowing for student control.

So What?: The Outcomes

Now that you've developed your skills, learned new information, and gained insights, what are you going to do?
- What is your take-away in terms of the texts, standards, and essential questions? Then, decide what information needs to be shared so that you can convey your knowledge to the class and how you are going to do it. When we discuss this as a class I will expect you to discuss the process as well as the information you found. Was there something you found difficult? Did you learn anything about yourself? If you had to start over what would you do differently?
- How does the research you completed fit with the research completed by others in the class? What picture does it paint of Nazi Germany?
- Finally, what was left out?

FIGURE 91. "So what?" from the Holocaust studies ILP. Reproduced with permission from Dan Butler.

Conclusion

The ILP is a way for students to take responsibility for their learning, and that is something that anyone can try, even if it's with one small activity. You certainly don't have to ditch everything you do to apply the tenets of this practice; giving control to students might start with allowing them to design a single activity or selecting a text to add to the current class's study. You simply have to consider what you're willing to let go of and what you want to maintain control over—and why.

A senior student once commented that he liked this approach because he wasn't limited to his teacher's knowledge base. He explained that, in his other classes, he could only learn what the teacher knew, but, with this model, he had the ability to learn things that weren't even on the teacher's radar. We are no longer the dispensers of information that we were in our previous, more traditional classrooms. And, although we have had to let go of students loving what we loved about our favorite texts or understanding concepts near and dear to our hearts, we have begun to see much deeper and more meaningful learning for our students.

We interviewed our supervisor, Brendan McIsaac, after he co-taught one of the ILP courses and observed our classes many times. He offered this advice to teachers who might like to try this for the first time:

> Be brave, and be flexible . . . the flexibility being both on the part of the teacher, just the willingness to let go and hand things over to the kids, and . . . with the supervisors or administrators allowing teachers to have the latitude and room to experiment, recognizing that it may not fit the traditional mold . . . but I think ultimately what is gained there is something that is a benefit to everyone. (2012)

If you are ready to be brave and be flexible, you will soon find that your students are too. Just wait until you see what they discover and how much they can teach you as you let go.

For additional information, please see the online appendix at lettinggo-book .com and use the password #ncteILP815 for access.

Works Cited

Abrams, J. J. (Writer & Director), & Lindelof, D. (Writer). (2004). Pilot [Television series episode]. In J. J. Abrams (Executive producer), *Lost*. Santa Monica, CA: Bad Robot Productions.

American Association of School Librarians (AASL). (2007). *Standards for the 21st century learner*. Chicago: American Association of School Librarians.

Atwell, N. (1987). *In the middle: Writing, reading, and learning with adolescents*. Portsmouth, NH: Heinemann.

Barron, B., & Darling-Hammond, L. (2008). How can we teach for meaningful learning? In L. Darling-Hammond (Ed.), *Powerful learning: What we know about teaching for understanding*. San Francisco: Jossey-Bass.

Beers, G. K., & Probst, R. E. (2012). *Notice & note: Strategies for close reading*. Portsmouth, NH: Heinemann.

Bloom, B. S. (Ed.). (1956). *Taxonomy of educational objectives: The classification of educational goals by a committee of college and university examiners*. Handbook I: Cognitive domain. New York: David McKay Company.

Burke, J. (2010). *What's the big idea? Question-driven units to motivate reading, writing, and thinking*. Portsmouth, NH: Heinemann.

Burke, J. (2014). The A-list: Essential academic words. Retrieved from https://us.corwin.com/sites/default/files/upm-binaries/67396_Burke_AcademicMoves_IFC_FINAL.pdf

Common Core State Standards Initiative (CCSSI). (2010). *Common core state standards for English language arts and literacy in history/social studies, science, and technical subjects*. Retrieved from http://www.corestandards.org/ELA-Literacy/

Costa, A. L. (2008). Chapter 2: Describing the habits of mind. In A. L. Costa & B. Kallick (Eds.), *Learning and leading with habits of mind: 16 essential characteristics for success*. Alexandria, VA: Association for Supervision and Curriculum Development. Retrieved from http://www.ascd.org/publications/books/108008/chapters/Describing-the-Habits-of-Mind.aspx

Crockett, L., Jukes, I., & Churches, A. (2011). *Literacy is not enough: 21st century fluencies for the digital age*. Kelowna, British Columbia, Canada: 21st Century Fluency Project.

Cushman, K. (2010). *Fires in the mind: What kids can tell us about motivation and mastery.* San Francisco: Jossey-Bass.

Cushman, K. (2014, February 25). "Tell me more" as a way into student engagement [Blog post]. Retrieved from http://dlmooc.deeper-learning.org/tell-me-more/

Deresiewicz, W. (2014). *Excellent sheep: The miseducation of the American elite and the way to a meaningful life.* New York: Free Press.

Dewey, J. (1916). *Democracy and education: An introduction to the philosophy of education.* New York: Macmillan.

Donhauser, M., Hersey, H., Stutzman, C., & Zane, M. (2014a). From lesson plan to learning plan: An introduction to the inquiry learning plan. *School Library Monthly* (an imprint of ABC-CLIO), *31*(1), 11–13.

Donhauser, M., Hersey, H., Stutzman, C., & Zane, M. (2014b). Inquiry learning: The starting point. *School Library Monthly* (an imprint of ABC-CLIO), *31*(2), 8–10.

Donhauser, M., Hersey, H., Stutzman, C., & Zane, M. (2015a). The inquiry learning plan: Creating engaging questions. *School Library Monthly* (an imprint of ABC-CLIO), *31*(3), 8–10.

Donhauser, M., Hersey, H., Stutzman, C., & Zane, M. (2015b). The inquiry learning plan: The role of standards. *School Library Monthly* (an imprint of ABC-CLIO), *31*(4), 8–11.

Donhauser, M., Hersey, H., Stutzman, C., & Zane, M. (2015c). The role of reflection in the inquiry plan. *School Library Monthly* (an imprint of ABC-CLIO), *31*(6), 8–10.

Donhauser, M., Hersey, H., Stutzman, C., & Zane, M. (2015d). Final product assessment: So what? *School Library Monthly* (an imprint of ABC-CLIO), *31*(7), 8–11.

Downes, S. (2011, May 25). A world to change [Blog post]. Retrieved from https://www.huffingtonpost.com/stephen-downes/a-world-to-change_b_762738.html

Eisen, P. S. (2007). Yo Socrates! Amend this! *School Library Media Activities Monthly, 24*(2), 18–21.

Gardner, H. (n.d.). The components of MI. Retrieved from http://multipleintelligencesoasis.org/about/the-components-of-mi/

Green, J., & Green, H. (Producers, Presenters). (n.d.) *Crash Course* [YouTube Channel]. Retrieved from https://thecrashcourse.com/

Harvey, S., & Daniels, H. (2009). *Comprehension and collaboration: Inquiry circles in action.* Portsmouth, NH: Heinemann.

International Society for Technology in Education. (2008). *National educational technology standards for teachers* (2nd ed.). Washington, DC: International Society for Technology in Education.

Juliani, A. J. (2014). The complete guide to 20% time (and genius hour) in the classroom. Retrieved from http://ajjuliani.com/20-time-guide/

Kesler, C. (2016, August 5). What is genius hour? [Blog post]. Retrieved from http://www.keslerscience.com/what-is-genius-hour/

Kittle, P. (2012). *Book love: Developing depth, stamina, and passion in adolescent readers.* Portsmouth, NH: Heinemann.

Kohn, A. (2004). *What does it mean to be well educated? And more essays on standards, grading, and other follies*. Boston: Beacon Press.

Kuhlthau, C. C. (2004). *Seeking meaning: A process approach to library and information services* (2nd ed.). Westport, CT: Libraries Unlimited.

Kuhlthau, C. C., Maniotes, L. K., & Caspari, A. K. (2012). *Guided inquiry design: A framework for inquiry in your school*. Santa Barbara, CA: Libraries Unlimited.

Kuhlthau, C. C., Maniotes, L. K., & Caspari, A. K. (2015). *Guided inquiry: Learning in the 21st century* (2nd ed.). Santa Barbara, CA: Libraries Unlimited.

Lehmann, C. (2013, February 19). School must be real life [Blog post]. Retrieved from http://practicaltheory.org/blog/2013/02/19/school-must-be-real-life/

Maniotes, L. K. (Ed.) (2017). *Guided inquiry design in action: High school*. Santa Barbara, CA: Libraries Unlimited.

Martin-Kniep, G. O., & Picone-Zocchia, J. (2009). *Changing the way you teach, improving the way students learn*. Alexandria, VA: Association for Supervision and Curriculum Development.

Marzano, R., Pickering, D., & Pollock, J. E. (2001). *Classroom instruction that works: Research-based strategies for increasing student achievement*. Alexandria, VA: Association for Supervision and Curriculum Development.

McCombs, B. (n.d.). Developing responsible and autonomous learners: A key to motivating students. Retrieved from http://www.apa.org/education/k12/learners.aspx

McIsaac, B. (Presenter). (2012, November 14). *Inquiry Learning: Support from Admin, Teachers, & Parents* [Video file]. Retrieved from http://lettinggo-book.com/videos/

McTighe, J., & Wiggins, G. P. (2013). *Essential questions: Opening doors to student understanding*. Alexandria, VA: Association for Supervision and Curriculum Development.

Medina, J. (2008). *Brain rules: 12 principles for surviving and thriving at work, home, and school*. Seattle: Pear Press.

Moss, C. M., Brookhart, S. M., & Long, B. A. (2011). Knowing your learning target. *Educational Leadership, 68*(6), 66–69.

NCTE. (2013). *NCTE framework for 21st century curriculum and assessment*. Retrieved from http://www2.ncte.org/statement/21stcentframework/

NCTE & International Reading Association. (1996). *Standards for the English language arts*. Retrieved from http://www.ncte.org/library/NCTEFiles/Resources/Books/Sample/StandardsDoc.pdf

Richardson, W. (2012). *Why school? How education must change when learning and information are everywhere* [Kindle edition]. New York: TED Conferences.

Smith, M. W., Appleman, D., & Wilhelm, J. D. (2014). *Uncommon core: Where the authors of the standards go wrong about instruction—and how you can get it right*. Thousand Oaks, CA: Corwin Literacy.

Smith, M. W., Wilhelm, J. D., & Fredricksen, J. E. (2012). *Oh, yeah?! Putting argument to work both in school and out*. Portsmouth, NH: Heinemann.

Sollner, E. (Presenter). (2012, November 14). *Inquiry Learning: Support from Admin, Teachers, & Parents* [Video file]. Retrieved from http://lettinggo-book.com/videos/

Sollner, E. (Presenter). (2014, July 7). *Teacher's role in inquiry classroom* [Video file]. Retrieved from http://lettinggo-book.com/videos/

TEDx Talks. (2010, April 17). *TEDxNYED - Chris Lehmann - 03/06/10* [Video file]. Retrieved from https://www.youtube.com/watch?v=6FEMCyHYTyQ

Valenza, J. K. (2004). *Power tools recharged: 125+ essential forms and presentations for your school library information program.* Chicago: American Library Association.

Warrell, M. (2013, April 22). Why getting comfortable with discomfort is crucial to success. *Forbes.* Retrieved from http://www.forbes.com/sites/margiewarrell/2013/04/22/is-comfort-holding-you-back/

Weimer, M. (2014, September 10). "She didn't teach. We had to learn it ourselves" [Blog post]. Retrieved from http://www.facultyfocus.com/articles/teaching-professor-blog/didnt-teach-learn/#sthash.X4YipyrZ.dpuf

Wheatley, M. J. (2002). *Turning to one another: Simple conversations to restore hope to the future.* San Francisco: Berrett-Koehler Publishers.

Wiggins, G. (2013, December 5). Mandating the mere posting of objectives, and other pointless ideas [Blog post]. Retrieved from https://grantwiggins.wordpress.com/2013/12/05/mandating-the-daily-posting-of-objectives-and-other-dumb-ideas/

Wiggins, G. P., & McTighe, J. (2005). *Understanding by design* (2nd ed.). Alexandria, VA: Association for Supervision and Curriculum Development.

Wilhelm, J. D. (2007). *Engaging readers & writers with inquiry: Promoting deep understandings in language arts and the content areas with guiding questions.* New York: Scholastic.

Index

Authors

Meg Donhauser is an English teacher at Hunterdon Central Regional High School in Flemington, New Jersey. After graduating from Rutgers College and The College of New Jersey, she sought meaningful learning opportunities for her students. She first designed and implemented the ILP in the Fall of 2010 with a brave group of British literature students, who paved the way for hundreds of others to take control of their learning. Since then, she has collaborated extensively with Heather and Cathy, presenting their work at  state and national conferences, such as the NCTE Annual Convention and the AASL National Conference, and publishing in *School Library Monthly*, *The English Record*, and *The New Jersey English Journal*. She continues to learn as both a teacher and student, focusing on instruction and leadership. Along with Cathy, Heather, and Brien Gorham, she is also coauthor of the book *Nobody Does It Alone: Whispers from the LOST Community* (2014).

Heather Hersey has been a teacher librarian at Lakeside School in Seattle since September 2011 after moving from New Jersey, where she worked at Hunterdon Central Regional High School as a librarian for eight years and an English teacher for three years. She has an MA in English from Seton Hall University and an MEd in English Education from Rutgers University, where she also completed her master's in library science in 2006. Her love of reading, especially science fiction and fantasy, drew her to librarianship, but it  was her interest in the inquiry process and how students search for and use information that made becoming a librarian irresistible. She has published articles in journals such as *School Library Monthly* and *Learning & Leading with Technology*. Most recently, she published a chapter about research conferences in *Guided Inquiry Design in Action: High School* (Maniotes, 2017). She believes that questions are way more important than answers and hopes to instill this mind-set in all her students.

Cathy Stutzman is a teacher of English at Hunterdon Central Regional High School in Flemington, New Jersey. A graduate of Rutgers University's Graduate School of Education with over fifteen years of experience, she teaches a range of classes from AP and honors to college prep and in-class support. Cathy was a Communities for Learning Fellow from 2010 to 2013, during which time she explored ways to invite and honor student voice in all aspects of education. Her simultaneous collaboration with Meg and Heather  transformed her teaching into an approach that is rich with student inquiry and agency. Along with Meg and Heather, she has presented her work at state and national conferences, including the NCTE Annual Convention, and has published articles in *School Library Monthly*, *The English Record*, and *The New Jersey English Journal*. Cathy prides herself on learning alongside her students every day, and she is excited to share her learning here.

This book was typeset in TheMix and Palatino by Barbara Frazier.

Typefaces used on the cover include Egyptian Slate and Gill Sans.

The book was printed on 50-lb. White Offset paper by Versa Press, Inc.